30 Whole Foods Instant Pot Cookbook For Beginners

Simple, Yummy and Cleansing Instant Pot
Recipes For Effortless Results & Quick Detox

Kian Burton

CONTENTS

INTRODUCTION 8

POULTRY RECIPES...11

Chicken in Roasted Red Pepper Sauce 11

Instant Whole Chicken 12

Chicken with Mushrooms and Leeks 13

Herbed and Garlicky Chicken Wings 14

Mexican Chicken 15

Chicken with Red Potatoes and Green Beans...........................16

Coconut Chicken with Tomatoes.......................................17

Sweet Potato & Chicken Curry..18

Creamy Southern Chicken 19

Chicken with Water Chestnuts 20

Chicken Enchilada Soup 20

Turkey with Fennel and Celery.......................................21

Stewed Chicken with Kale 22

Pear and Onion Goose 23

Duck and Green Pea Soup...24

RED MEAT RECIPES 25

Pork Shoulder in a Date BBQ Sauce 25

Brussel Sprout Pork Chops with Onions...............................26

Pork & Cabbage Soup with Veggies....................................27

Orange & Cinnamon Pork 28

Rutabaga & Apple Pork 29

Apple Pork Ribs..30

Citrusy Beef.. 30

Beef Ragu 31

Beef Pot Roast with Carrots 32

Beef Coconut Curry..33

Beef & Tomato Soup..34

Herbed Beef & Yams..34

Lamb Habanero Chili..36

Lamb Stew with Apricots 37

Mutton with Potatoes and Tomatoes 38

FISH AND SEAFOOD RECIPES 39

Tilapia Chowder.. 39

Salmon with Broccoli and Potatoes................................40

Veggie Noodle Salmon 41

Sea Bass Stew 42

Crab Cakes 43

VEGAN AND VEGETARIAN RECIPES 44

Potato Chili.. 44

Potato and Spinach Bowl 45

Root Veggie Casserole 46

Coconut and Zucchini Soup 46

Lime & Mint Zoodles 47

Walnut & Cinnamon Sweet Potatoes...............................48

Zucchini Coconut Burgers 48

Cauliflower Tabbouleh with Mint and Parsley........................49

Potato & Leek Patties 50

Cabbage, Beet & Apple Stew.....................................50

Basil and Tomato "Pasta" 51

Squash and Sweet Potato Lunch Soup.................................52

Tomato and Kale "Rice" 52

Beet Borscht 53

Veggie Flax Burgers...54

VEGETABLES AND SIDE DISHES............................ 55

Classic Mashed Potatoes 55

Garlic & Herb Potatoes 56

Lime Cabbage with Coconut...57

Turmeric Carrot Mash...58

Simple Steamed Potatoes...59

Creamy Potato and Scallion Salad...60

Cabbage, Pear, and Onion Side...61

Cauliflower and Pea Bowl...62

Stewed Yams with Zucchini...63

Potatoes and Green Beans 64

Lemony Rutabaga and Green Onion Salad 65

Garlicky Sweet Potato Mash...66

Pea and Sweet Potato Bowl...67

Orange Potatoes with Walnuts 68

Garlicky Zucchini and Carrot Noodles...69

FAST SNACKS AND APPETIZERS............................ 70

Chili Hash Browns...70

Nutty Carrot Sticks...71

Paprika Potato Slices...72

Salty and Peppery Sweet Potato Snack...73

Garlicky Pepper and Tomato Appetizer...74

Porcini and Sesame Dip...74

Lemony Cippolini Onions...75

Pico de Gallo with Carrots..76

Tahini, Carrot, and Spinach "Hummus".....................................76

Jalapeno and Pineapple Salsa 77

Balsamic Carrots 78

Turnip and Sultana Dip with Pecans 79

Pea and Avocado Dip 80

Turmeric Sweet Potato Sticks...81

Tropical Salsa Mash...82

BREAKFAST RECIPES.. 83

Almond & Gala Apple Porridge 83

Carrot & Pecan Muffins 84

Kale, Tomato & Carrot Quiche 85

Sweet Potato & Carrot Egg Casserole.......................................86

Onion and Tomato Eggs 87

Bell Pepper & Onion Frittata 88

Egg and Beef Casserole with Kale and Leek 89

Easy Soft-Boiled Eggs...90

Pear, Coconut & Walnut Porridge 90

Eggs & Smoked Salmon..91

DESSERT RECIPES 92

Cinnamon and Lemon Apples..92

Chocolate and Almond Banana Squares 93

Very Berry Cream...94

Coconut Pear Delight...94

Creamy Almond and Coconut Apple Dessert..............................95

Almond Pear Wedges 96

Black Currant Poached Peaches 96

Apple and Peach Compote...97

Tutty Fruity Sauce 98

Almond Butter Bananas 99

CONCLUSION...100

INTRODUCTION

Taking the healthy plunge and choosing a balanced diet free of the dietary hazards can bring many benefits your way. In a world where food is the number one culprit for the development of many diseases, switching to a healthy diet is the best way to grant yourself the ticket for a hale and hearty retirement. But before you choose whether to ditch the carbs or the fats and decide on a more permanent dietary plan, you need to cleanse your body first in order to prepare it for a healthier lifestyle.

There are many detoxifying plans that can help you do that, however, the most popular and most successful way to hit the reset button is to go 30 Days Whole Foods.

Revealing to you the concept of 30 Days Whole Foods, how to start this challenge, and what to fill your tummy with for a month, this book is the best guide that can steer you in a healthy dietary direction.

Offering you 100 mouthwatering 30 Days Whole Foods recipes that can be prepared in a jiffy in your Instant Pot, this book will show you that there is absolutely nothing challenging about following the 30 Days Whole Foods challenge. Want to see how healthy, delicious, and cleansing can go together? Jump to the first recipe and let your tummy be the judge of that. You will not be disappointed!

Going 30 Days Whole Foods

If you are considering to start to follow a healthier dietary plan then you must have heard about the 30 Days Whole Foods challenge. Since 2009, millions of people have actually restored their health thanks to the amazing 30 Days Whole Foods program. But what does this challenge actually entail? Will you be forced to tracking every morsel that goes into your mouth for a month? Or can you actually rebalance your health and metabolism with a full tummy?

What Is 30 Days Whole Foods?

30 Days Whole Foods is a fast, 30-day diet plan that can help you restore your health, heal your digestive tract, bring balance back to your tummy, and actually help you lose weight, all by purging certain food groups from your diet.

You may not be aware of this, but there are certain foods (such as grains or dairy) that may be causing inflammation, unbalancing your hormones, and disrupting your entire metabolism. By excluding such foods from your diet completely, you will reset your diet and cleanse your body. And all in just 30 days.

What Are the Forbidden Food Groups?

The point of the 30 Days Whole Foods challenge is to strip your diet from these potential hazards in order to rebalance your gut:

- Grains
- Beans and Legumes
- All Dairy Products (milk, cheese, yogurt, cream, etc.)
- Processed Meat
- All Forms of Sugar (white and brown sugar, maple syrup, honey, agave nectar, etc.)
- Artificial Sweeteners
- Baked Goods
- Processed Meat
- All Processed Foods

Are There Any Exceptions?

The only exception here is that you can actually eat green beans and green peas. Even though, technically, they are legumes, this challenge includes them in this diet so feel free to safely incorporate them into your meals.

What Should You Eat?

As the name 30 Days Whole Foods suggests, you should consume only whole and unprocessed foods. When you strip away the previously mentioned forbidden foods, these are the foods that are safe to consume on 30 Days Whole Foods:

- Fresh Vegetables

- Fresh Fruits

- Unprocessed Meat, in moderation

- Fish and Shellfish

- Eggs

- Seeds

- Nuts

- Nut Milk and Nut Flour

- Coconut Oil, Olive Oil, Ghee

How to Make the Most Out of This Challenge?

In order for you to make the most out of this challenge is to simply follow the rules. That means, no munching on the forbidden items and eating only the Whole 30-compliant ingredients. But, it is also important to get the point of this challenge. The point here is to strip away all of the unhealthy, junk foods, not to try to recreate them with healthier ingredients. So, no to baking cakes with nut flours, no to trying to enjoy a juicy burger with a grain-free bun. The point here is to cleanse your body completely.

If you are craving a dessert, just get creative with fruit. This book offers 10 fruity dessert recipes that will give you a great idea on how to "survive" these 30 days without sacrificing your satisfied taste buds.

POULTRY RECIPES

Chicken in Roasted Red Pepper Sauce

PREPARATION TIME: 10 minutes **COOKING TIME:** 13 minutes **SERVES:** 6

INGREDIENTS:

1 ½ pounds Chicken Breasts, cubed
1 Onion, diced
4 Garlic Cloves
12 ounces Roasted Red Peppers
2 tsp Adobo Sauce
1 tbsp Apple Cider Vinegar

1 tsp Cumin
Juice of ½ Lemon
3 tbsp chopped Cilantro
1 tbsp Olive Oil
Salt and Pepper, to taste

INSTRUCTIONS:

Place the garlic, red pepper, adobo sauce, lemon juice, vinegar, cilantro, and some salt and pepper, in your food processor. Process until the mixture becomes smooth.

Set your Instant Pot to "SAUTE" and heat the olive oil in it.

Add the onion and cook for 2 minutes.

Add the chicken cubes and cook until they are no longer pink. Pour the sauce over and close the lid. Turn it clockwise to seal and then hit the "MANUAL" button.

Set the cooking time to 8 minutes and cook on HIGH pressure.

After you hear the beeping sound, press "KEEP WARM/CANCEL". Move the pressure handle to "Venting" for a quick pressure release and open the lid carefully. Serve and enjoy!

NUTRITION FACTS PER SERVING:

Calories 205, Protein 32g, Total Carbs 1g, Total Fat 8g, Saturated Fat 3g, Fiber 1g, Sodium 660mg

Instant Whole Chicken

PREPARATION TIME: 10 minutes **COOKING TIME:** 28 minutes **SERVES:** 8

INGREDIENTS:

3 - pound Whole Chicken

1 cup Chicken Broth

1 ½ tbsp Olive Oil

1 tsp Paprika

¾ tsp Garlic Powder

¼ tsp Onion Powder

INSTRUCTIONS:

Rinse the chicken well under cold water, remove the giblets, and pat it dry with some paper towels.

In a small bowl, combine the oil and spices.

Rub the chicken well with the mixture. Turn your Instant Pot on and set it to "SAUTE".

Add the chicken to it and sear on all sides until it becomes golden.

Pour the chicken broth around the chicken (not over it), and put the lid on. Turn it clockwise to seal and press the "MANUAL" button.

Set the cooking time to 25 minutes and cook on HIGH pressure.

When the timer goes off, select "KEEP WARM/CANCEL".

Move the pressure handle from "Sealing" to "Venting" for a quick pressure release.

Open the lid carefully.

Transfer the chicken to a platter and let sit for about 10 minutes before carving.

Serve and enjoy!

NUTRITION FACTS PER SERVING:

Calories 290, Protein 40g, Total Carbs 0.3g, Total Fat 10g, Saturated Fat 6g, Fiber 0g, Sodium 310mg

Chicken with Mushrooms and Leeks

PREPARATION TIME: 10 minutes **COOKING TIME:** 15 minutes **SERVES:** 6

INGREDIENTS:

2 pounds Chicken Breasts, cubed
4 tbsp Ghee
1 ¼ pounds Mushrooms, sliced
½ cup Chicken Broth
2 tbsp Arrowroot

½ cup Almond Milk
¼ tsp Black Pepper
2 Leeks, sliced
¼ tsp Garlic Powder

INSTRUCTIONS:

Turn your Instant Pot on and set it to "SAUTE". Add the ghee and wait until it is melted.

Place the chicken cubes inside and cook until they are no longer pink and become slightly golden in color. Transfer the chicken pieces to a plate.

Add the leeks and sliced mushrooms to the pot and cook for about 3 minutes. Return the chicken to the Instant Pot, season with pepper and garlic powder and pour the broth over.

Give the mixture a good stir to combine everything well, then close the lid. Turn it clockwise to seal and then hit the "MANUAL" button. Set the cooking time to 8 minutes and cook on HIGH pressure.

After the beeping sound, hit "KEEP WARM/CANCEL". Move the pressure handle from "Sealing" to "Venting" to release the pressure quickly.

Open the lid carefully. In a bowl, whisk together the almond milk and arrowroot. Pour the mixture over the chicken and set the Instant Pot to "SAUTE" again. Cook until the sauce becomes thickened.

Serve and enjoy!

NUTRITION FACTS PER SERVING:

Calories 550, Protein 49g, Total Carbs 37g, Total Fat 24g, Saturated Fat 12.5g, Fiber 3g, Sodium 630mg

Herbed and Garlicky Chicken Wings

PREPARATION TIME: 15 minutes **COOKING TIME:** 10 minutes **SERVES:** 4

INGREDIENTS:

12 Chicken Wings
¼ cup Chicken Broth
1 tbsp Basil
1 tbsp Oregano
½ tbsp Tarragon

1 tbsp minced Garlic
2 tbsp Olive Oil
¼ tsp Pepper
1 cup of Water

INSTRUCTIONS:

Pour the water into the Instant Pot and lower the rack.

Place all of the ingredients in a bowl and mix with your hands to combine well.

Cover the bowl and let the wings sit for about 15 minutes.

Arrange on the rack and close the lid of the Instant Pot. Turn it clockwise until you hear the chime that indicates proper sealing.

Select the "MANUAL" button and with the "+" and "-" buttons set the cooking time to 10 minutes. Cook on HIGH.

After the beep, select "KEEP WARM/CANCEL".

Move the pressure handle from "Sealing" to "Venting" in order to do a quick pressure release.

Open the lid carefully.

Serve the wings drizzled with the cooking liquid and enjoy!

NUTRITION FACTS PER SERVING:

Calories 160, Protein 14g, Total Carbs 0.6g, Total Fat 13g, Saturated Fat 8g, Fiber 0g, Sodium 300mg

Mexican Chicken

PREPARATION TIME: 10 minutes **COOKING TIME:** 20 minutes **SERVES:** 6

INGREDIENTS:

1 Red Bell Pepper, diced
1 Green Bell Pepper, diced
1 Jalapeno, diced
2 pounds Chicken Breasts
10 oz canned diced Tomatoes
1 Red Onion, diced

½ tsp Cumin
¾ tsp Chili Powder
¼ tsp Pepper
Juice of 1 Lime
¼ cup Chicken Broth
1 tbsp Olive Oil

INSTRUCTIONS:

Turn the Instant Pot on and heat the oil on "SAUTE". When sizzling, add the onion and bell peppers and cook for about 3-4 minutes, until the veggies become soft.

Add the remaining ingredients and give the mixture a good stir to combine. Close the lid and then turn it clockwise to seal. Press the "MANUAL" button.

Set the cooking time to 15 minutes and cook on HIGH pressure.

Press the "KEEP WARM/CANCEL" button after you hear the beep.

Move the pressure handle from "Sealing" to "Venting" to release the pressure quickly, but keep your hand away from the steam.

Open the lid carefully and grab two forks.

Shred the chicken inside the pot with the forks, and then stir to combine it with the juices.

Serve immediately. Enjoy!

NUTRITION FACTS PER SERVING:

Calories 340, Protein 43g, Total Carbs 11g, Total Fat 14g, Saturated Fat 6.5g, Fiber 1g, Sodium 245mg

Chicken with Red Potatoes and Green Beans

PREPARATION TIME: 5 minutes **COOKING TIME:** 22 minutes **SERVES:** 6

INGREDIENTS:

2 pounds Chicken Thighs

1 tbsp Ghee

¼ tsp dried Parsley

¼ tsp dried Oregano

½ tsp dried Thyme

Juice of 1 Lemon

½ cup Chicken Broth

2 tbsp Olive Oil

1 Garlic Clove, minced

1 pound Green Beans

1 pound Red Potatoes, halved

INSTRUCTIONS:

Turn your Instant Pot on and set it to "SAUTE". Add the oil and ghee and cook until the ghee becomes melted. Add the minced garlic and cook it for a minute.

Place the chicken thighs inside and cook them on both sides, until golden. Stir in the herbs and the lemon juice and cook for an additional minute, until fragrant.

Add all of the remaining ingredients and stir well to combine. Close the lid. Turn it clockwise to seal and then hit the "MANUAL" button. Set the cooking time to 15 minutes and cook on HIGH pressure.

After you hear the beep, select "KEEP WARM/CANCEL".

Move the pressure handle from "Sealing" to "Venting" to release the pressure quickly.

Open the lid carefully.

Serve immediately. Enjoy!

NUTRITION FACTS PER SERVING:

Calories 500, Protein 45g, Total Carbs 19g, Total Fat 27g, Saturated Fat 14g, Fiber 3g, Sodium 450mg

Coconut Chicken with Tomatoes

PREPARATION TIME: 10 minutes **COOKING TIME:** 17 minutes **SERVES:** 4

INGREDIENTS:

1 ½ pounds Chicken Thighs
1 ½ cups chopped Tomatoes
1 Onion, chopped
1 ½ tbsp Ghee
2 cups Coconut Milk
½ cup chopped Almonds
2 tsp Paprika

1 tsp Garam Masala
2 tbsp chopped Cilantro
1 tsp Turmeric
1 tsp Cayenne Powder
1 tsp Ginger Powder
1 ¼ tsp Garlic Powder
Salt and Pepper, to taste

INSTRUCTIONS:

Turn the Instant Pot on and set it to "SAUTE". Place the ghee inside and cook until it becomes melted.

Add the onions and saute until translucent, about 3 minutes or so.

Add all of the spices and cook for an additional minute, until fragrant. Stir in the tomatoes and coconut milk.

Place the chicken thighs inside and put the lid on. Seal by turning clockwise and set the cooking time to 13 minutes. Cook on "MANUAL" on HIGH pressure.

When the timer goes off, press the "KEEP WARM/CANCEL" button.

Move the pressure handle from "Sealing" to "Venting" for a quick pressure release and open the lid carefully.

Serve topped with chopped almonds and cilantro.

Enjoy!

NUTRITION FACTS PER SERVING:

Calories 270, Protein 19g, Total Carbs 28g, Total Fat 8g, Saturated Fat 2.2g, Fiber 2.2g, Sodium 625mg

Sweet Potato & Chicken Curry

PREPARATION TIME: 10 minutes **COOKING TIME:** 18 minutes **SERVES:** 4

INGREDIENTS:

1 pound Boneless and Skinless Chicken Breast, cubed

2 cups cubed Sweet Potatoes

2 cups Green Beans

½ Onion, chopped

1 Bell Pepper, sliced

1 ½ tsp minced Garlic

1 tsp Cumin

1 can Coconut Milk

2 tsp Ghee

3 tbsp Curry Powder

1 tsp Turmeric

⅔ cup Chicken Broth

Salt and Pepper, to taste

INSTRUCTIONS:

Turn the Instant Pot on and set it to "SAUTE".

Place the ghee inside and melt it. Add the onions and cook for about 3 minutes.

Add the garlic and cook for 30 seconds more.

Add the remaining ingredients, except the milk, to the pot. Stir well to combine and put the lid on.

Seal by turning clockwise and select the "MANUAL" cooking mode. Set the cooking time to 12 minutes. Cook on HIGH.

Hit the "KEEP WARM/CANCEL" button after the beep. Move the pressure handle to "Venting" for a quick pressure release and open the lid carefully.

Stir in the coconut milk and set the Instant Pot to "SAUTE" again. Cook for 3 minutes.

Serve immediately and enjoy!

NUTRITION FACTS PER SERVING:

Calories 330, Protein 26g, Total Carbs 19g, Total Fat 15g, Saturated Fat 8g, Fiber 4g, Sodium 445mg

Creamy Southern Chicken

PREPARATION TIME: 10 minutes **COOKING TIME:** 15 minutes **SERVES:** 5

INGREDIENTS:

1 ½ pounds Boneless Chicken Thighs
2 tsp Paprika
2 Bell Peppers, sliced
1 cup Chicken Broth
½ cup Coconut Milk
1 tbsp Chili Powder
¼ cup Lime Juice

1 tsp Cumin
½ tsp Garlic Powder
½ tsp Onion Powder
1 tsp Ground Coriander
½ tsp Cayenne Pepper
1 tbsp Olive Oil
1 tbsp Arrowroot

INSTRUCTIONS:

Turn the Instant Pot on and set it to "SAUTE". Add the olive oil to it and cook until hot and sizzling. Meanwhile, combine all of the spices in a small bowl and rub the mixture all over the chicken.

Add the chicken to the pot and cook until golden on both sides. Hit "CANCEL".

Pour the broth and lime juice over and stir in the peppers.

Close the lid. Seal by turning clockwise and select "MANUAL". By using the "+" and "-" buttons, set the cooking time to 7 minutes. Cook on HIGH pressure.

When the timer goes off, press the "KEEP WARM/CANCEL" button.

Move the pressure handle from "Sealing" to "Venting" for a quick pressure release and open the lid carefully.

Stir in the coconut milk and arrowroot and press "SAUTE". Cook until the sauce thickens.

Serve and enjoy!

NUTRITION FACTS PER SERVING:

Calories 290 , Protein 36g, Total Carbs 32g, Total Fat 8g, Saturated Fat 2g, Fiber 7g, Sodium 550mg

Chicken with Water Chestnuts

PREPARATION TIME: 5 minutes **COOKING TIME:** 10 minutes **SERVES:** 4

INGREDIENTS:

1 pound Ground Chicken
¼ cup Chicken Broth
2 tbsp Balsamic Vinegar

½ cup Water Chestnuts, sliced
¼ cup Coconut Aminos
Pinch of Allspice

INSTRUCTIONS:

Place all of the ingredients in your Instant Pot. Give the mixture a good stir to combine, and then put the lid on. Seal by turning clockwise and then press the "MANUAL" button. Set the cooking time to 10 minutes with the help of the "+" and "-" buttons. Cook on HIGH.

When the timer goes off, press the "KEEP WARM/CANCEL" button. Release the pressure quickly by turning the pressure handle from "Sealing" to "Venting". Open the lid very carefully and keep your hand away from the steam. Serve and enjoy!

NUTRITION FACTS PER SERVING:

Calories 270, Protein 33g, Total Carbs 11g, Total Fat 8.6g, Saturated Fat 1.5g, Fiber 3g, Sodium 330mg

Chicken Enchilada Soup

PREPARATION TIME: 10 minutes **COOKING TIME:** 20 minutes **SERVES:** 6

INGREDIENTS:

1 ½ pounds Chicken Breasts
1 tbsp Chili Powder
2 tsp minced Garlic
2 cups Chicken Broth
1 tbsp Cumin

½ tsp Smoked Paprika
1 tsp Oregano
14 ounces canned diced Tomatoes
1 Bell Pepper, sliced
1 Onion, sliced

INSTRUCTIONS:

Place all of the ingredients and ½ cup water in your Instant Pot. Stir well to combine everything and then put the lid of the Instant Pot on. Turn it clockwise to seal properly and select "MANUAL". By using the "+" and "-" buttons, set the cooking time to 20 minutes. Cook on HIGH pressure.

When the timer goes off, press the "KEEP WARM/CANCEL" button. Do not open the lid until the valve has dropped down. That allows the pressure to come out naturally. Open the lid carefully and ladle into bowls. Serve.

NUTRITION FACTS PER SERVING:

Calories 270 , Protein 36g, Total Carbs 9g, Total Fat 9.5g, Saturated Fat 3.5g, Fiber 2.5g, Sodium 470mg

Turkey with Fennel and Celery

PREPARATION TIME: 10 minutes **COOKING TIME:** 15 minutes **SERVES:** 6

INGREDIENTS:

2 pounds Boneless and Skinless Turkey Breast
1 cup chopped Fennel Bulb
1 cup chopped Celery (with leaves)

2 ¼ cup Veggie or Chicken Stock
¼ tsp Pepper
¼ tsp Garlic Powder

INSTRUCTIONS:

Dump all of the ingredients in your Instant Pot. Give it a good stir to incorporate everything well and then put the lid on. Turn it clockwise. Select "MANUAL" mode. Set the cooking time to 15 minutes and cook on HIGH.

When done, move the pressure handle from "Sealing" to "Venting" for a quick pressure release. Grab two forks and shred the turkey inside the pot.

NUTRITION FACTS PER SERVING:

Calories 250, Protein 32g, Total Carbs 5g, Total Fat 8g, Saturated Fat 2g, Fiber 1.5g, Sodium 330mg

Stewed Chicken with Kale

INGREDIENTS:

1 pound Ground Chicken

1 cup chopped Tomatoes

1 cup diced Onions

1 cup chopped Carrots

1 cup chopped Kale

½ cup chopped Celery

6 cups Chicken Broth

2 Thyme Sprigs

1 tbsp Olive Oil

1 tsp Red Pepper Flakes

10 ounces Potato Noodles (spiralized Potatoes)

INSTRUCTIONS:

Turn the Instant Pot on and set it to "SAUTE". Add the oil and cook until it becomes hot and sizzling. Add the chicken and cook until it becomes golden. Stir in the onions, carrots, and celery, and cook for about 5 minutes. Stir in the remaining ingredients, except the noodles, and close the lid. Select the "MANUAL" cooking mode. Set the cooking time to 6 minutes. Cook on HIGH pressure.

When the timer goes off, press the "KEEP WARM/CANCEL" button. Move the pressure handle from "Sealing" to "Venting" for a quick pressure release and open the lid carefully. Stir in the potato noodles and close the lid again. Turn it clockwise to seal and click on "MANUAL" again. This time, cook for 4 minutes on HIGH.

Again, press "KEEP WARM/CANCEL" after the beep and do a quick pressure release. Open the lid and ladle into serving bowls. Enjoy!

NUTRITION FACTS PER SERVING:

Calories 240 , Protein 24g, Total Carbs 16g, Total Fat 8g, Saturated Fat 1.5g, Fiber 4g, Sodium 300mg

Pear and Onion Goose

PREPARATION TIME: 10 minutes **COOKING TIME:** 25 minutes **SERVES:** 6

INGREDIENTS:

1 cup Chicken Broth

1 tbsp Ghee

½ cup slice Onions

1 ½ pounds Goose, chopped into large pieces

2 tbsp Balsamic Vinegar

1 tsp Cayenne Pepper

3 Pears, peeled and sliced

¼ tsp Garlic Powder

½ tsp Pepper

INSTRUCTIONS:

Turn the Instant Pot on and set it to "SAUTE".

Add the ghee. When melted, add the goose and cook until it becomes golden on all sides.

Transfer to a plate.

Add the onions and cook for 2 minutes. Return the goose to the pot and add the rest of the ingredients.

Stir well to combine and close the lid. Turn it clockwise so it is sealed properly. Select the "MANUAL" cooking mode.

Set the cooking time to 18 minutes. Cook on HIGH pressure.

When the timer goes off, press the "KEEP WARM/CANCEL" button.

Move the pressure handle from "Sealing" to "Venting" for a quick pressure release.

Open the lid carefully.

Serve and enjoy!

NUTRITION FACTS PER SERVING:

Calories 290 , Protein 38.5g, Total Carbs 13g, Total Fat 7.5g, Saturated Fat 2.3g, Fiber 2g, Sodium 220mg

Duck and Green Pea Soup

PREPARATION TIME: 5 minutes **COOKING TIME:** 27 minutes **SERVES:** 6

INGREDIENTS:

1 cup diced Carrots

4 cups Veggie or Chicken Stock

1 pound Duck Breasts, chopped

20 ounces diced canned Tomatoes

1 cup chopped Celery

18 ounces Green Peas

1 cup diced Onions

2 Garlic Cloves, minced

1 tsp dried Marjoram

½ tsp Pepper

½ tsp Salt

INSTRUCTIONS:

Place all of the ingredients, except the peas, in your Instant Pot.

Stir well to combine and close the lid. Seal by turning clockwise.

Select the "SOUP" cooking mode and set the cooking time to 20 minutes.

After the beep, press the "KEEP WARM/CANCEL" button.

Move the pressure handle from "Sealing" to "Venting" for a quick pressure release and open the lid carefully. Stir in the peas.

Close the lid again but do NOT turn the Instant Pot on.

Let blanch for about 7 minutes. Ladle into serving bowls.

Enjoy!

NUTRITION FACTS PER SERVING:

Calories 240 , Protein 27g, Total Carbs 22g, Total Fat 4g, Saturated Fat 1g, Fiber 5g, Sodium 520mg

RED MEAT RECIPES

Pork Shoulder in a Date BBQ Sauce

PREPARATION TIME: 10 minutes **COOKING TIME:** 90 minutes **SERVES:** 8

INGREDIENTS:

4 pounds Pork Shoulder
1 tbsp Onion Powder
1 tbsp Garlic Powder
1 tbsp Pepper
1 tbsp Chili Powder

2 cups Chicken Stock
Sauce:
6 Dates, soaked
¼ cup Tomato Paste
½ cup Coconut Aminos

INSTRUCTIONS:

In a small bowl combine the onion powder, garlic powder, pepper, and chili powder. Rub the mixture into the pork. Place the pork inside your Instant Pot.

Pour the broth around the meat NOT over it, and then close the lid. Select the "MANUAL" cooking mode and set the cooking time to 90 minutes. Cook on HIGH pressure.

Meanwhile, place all of the sauce ingredients in a food processor and pulse until the mixture becomes smooth.

Select "KEEP WARM/CANCEL" after you hear the beep. Turn the pressure handle from "Sealing" to "Venting" to release the pressure quickly and open the lid carefully.

Grab two forks and shred the meat inside the pot. Pour the sauce over and stir to combine.

Serve a desired and enjoy!

NUTRITION FACTS PER SERVING:

Calories 420, Protein 33g, Total Carbs 47g, Total Fat 12g, Saturated Fat 5.2g, Fiber 3g, Sodium 700mg

Brussel Sprout Pork Chops with Onions

PREPARATION TIME: 10 minutes **COOKING TIME:** 28 minutes **SERVES:** 4

INGREDIENTS:

1 pound Pork Chops
1 cup sliced Onions
1 cup sliced Carrots
1 tbsp Ghee
2 cups Brussel Sprouts

1 tbsp Arrowroot
1 tsp minced Garlic
1 cup Chicken Stock
½ tsp dried Thyme

INSTRUCTIONS:

Turn the Instant Pot on and set it to "SAUTE". Add the ghee and cook until it becomes melted. Add the chops to the pot and cook on both sides until they become golden in color. Transfer them to a plate.

Add the onions to the Instant Pot and cook them for 3 minutes before adding the garlic. Saute for one more minute. Return the pork chops to the pot and pour the broth over.

Close the lid and choose the "MANUAL" cooking mode. Set the cooking time to 15 minutes. Cook on HIGH pressure.

When the timer goes off, press the "KEEP WARM/CANCEL" button. Move the pressure handle from "Sealing" to "Venting" for a quick pressure release and open the lid carefully. Stir in the carrots and Brussel sprouts. Close and seal the lid again. Choose "MANUAL" and cook for 3 minutes on HIGH.

Again, do a quick pressure release and open the lid. Transfer the chops and veggies to a serving platter. Whisk the arrowroot into the pot and cook on "SAUTE" until it becomes thickened.

Pour the sauce over the chops and veggies. Serve immediately and enjoy!

NUTRITION FACTS PER SERVING:

Calories 440, Protein 29g, Total Carbs 13g, Total Fat 32g, Saturated Fat 17g, Fiber 2g, Sodium 800mg

Pork & Cabbage Soup with Veggies

PREPARATION TIME: 10 minutes **COOKING TIME:** 15 minutes **SERVES:** 6

INGREDIENTS:

1 pound Ground Pork

1 Onion, diced

2 pounds Napa Cabbage, chopped

1 Potato, diced

6 Button Mushrooms, sliced

3 Scallions, sliced

2 Carrots, chopped

1 tbsp Ghee

4-6 cups Chicken Broth

Salt and Pepper, to taste

INSTRUCTIONS:

Turn the Instant Pot on and set it to "SAUTE". Melt the ghee in it and then add the pork.

Cook until it becomes browned, while breaking it with a spatula.

Once browned, add the onions and mushrooms and cook for another 4-5 minutes. Season with some salt and pepper.

Pour the chicken broth over and stir in the remaining ingredients.

Close the lid and turn clockwise to seal.

Select the "MANUAL" cooking mode. Set the cooking time to 6 minutes. Cook on HIGH pressure.

When the timer goes off, press the "KEEP WARM/CANCEL" button.

Turn the pressure handle to "Venting" for a quick pressure release and open the lid carefully.

Ladle into serving bowls immediately.

Enjoy!

NUTRITION FACTS PER SERVING:

Calories 305, Protein 26g, Total Carbs 12g, Total Fat 15g, Saturated Fat 7g, Fiber 3g, Sodium 625mg

Orange & Cinnamon Pork

PREPARATION TIME: 15 minutes **COOKING TIME:** 45 minutes **SERVES:** 10

INGREDIENTS:

2 tbsp Olive Oil
5 pounds Pork Shoulder
1 Cinnamon Stick
2 cups Fresh Orange Juice
1 tbsp Cumin
½ tsp Garlic Powder

¼ tsp Onion Powder
1 Onion, chopped
1 Jalapeno Pepper, diced
2 tsp Thyme
½ tsp Oregano
½ tsp Pepper

INSTRUCTIONS:

Place half of the oil in a small bowl. Add all of the spices and stir well to combine the mixture. Rub it all over the meat, making sure that the pork is well-coated.

Turn the Instant Pot on and set it to "SAUTE".

Add the remaining olive oil and heat it until hot. Add the pork and sear it on all sides until browned. Transfer to a plate.

Pour the orange juice into the pan and deglaze the bottom with a spatula.

Add the rest of the ingredients and stir to combine well. Return the pork to the pot. Close the lid and turn clockwise to seal.

Select the "MANUAL" cooking mode. Set the cooking time to 40 minutes. Cook on HIGH pressure.

When the timer goes off, press the "KEEP WARM/CANCEL" button. Let the pressure drop naturally by allowing the valve to come down on its own. Once the pressure has been released, open the lid. Grab two forks and shred the pork inside the pot. Stir to combine with the juices. Serve and enjoy!

NUTRITION FACTS PER SERVING:

Calories 750, Protein 55g, Total Carbs 14g, Total Fat 55g, Saturated Fat 28g, Fiber 3g, Sodium 780mg

Rutabaga & Apple Pork

PREPARATION TIME: 15 minutes **COOKING TIME:** 23 minutes **SERVES:** 4

INGREDIENTS:

1 tbsp Olive Oil
1 pound Pork Loin, cut into cubes
2 Apples, peeled and chopped
2 Rutabaga, peeled and chopped
1 Onion, diced
1 Celery Stalk, diced

1 tbsp chopped Parsley
½ cup sliced Leeks
1 ½ cups Beef Broth
½ tsp Cumin
½ tsp Thyme

INSTRUCTIONS:

Turn the Instant Pot on and set it to "SAUTE". Add half of the olive oil to it. When hot and sizzling, add the beef. Cook until it becomes browned on all sides. Transfer the cooked beef to a plate.

Add the leeks, onions, celery, and drizzle with the remaining oil. Stir to combine and cook for 3 minutes.

Add the beef back to the pot, pour the broth over, and stir in all of the herbs and spices. Close the lid and turn clockwise to seal. Select the "MANUAL" cooking mode. Set the cooking time to 10 minutes and cook on HIGH pressure.

After the beep, select "KEEP WARM/CANCEL". Turn the pressure handle to "Venting" for a quick pressure release and open the lid carefully. Stir in the rutabaga and apples.

Close the lid again and set the cooking time to 5 minutes. Again, cook on high pressure.

Do a quick pressure release once again, open the lid carefully, and serve immediately. Enjoy!

NUTRITION FACTS PER SERVING:

Calories 420, Protein 44g, Total Carbs 2g, Total Fat 24g, Saturated Fat 12g, Fiber 1g, Sodium 410mg

Apple Pork Ribs

PREPARATION TIME: 10 minutes **COOKING TIME:** 30 minutes **SERVES:** 4

INGREDIENTS:

½ cup Apple Cider Vinegar

2 pounds Pork Ribs

3 ½ cups Apple Juice

INSTRUCTIONS:

Pour the apple juice and the apple cider vinegar into the Instant Pot and lower the trivet. Place the pork ribs on top of the trivet and then close the lid. Turn it clockwise to seal properly. After the chime, choose the "MANUAL" cooking mode. Set the cooking time to 30 minutes. Cook on HIGH pressure.

After the beep, press the "KEEP WARM/CANCEL" button. Let the valve drop on its own for a natural pressure release. Open the lid carefully. Serve.

NUTRITION FACTS PER SERVING:

Calories 504, Protein 39g, Total Carbs 25g, Total Fat 28g, Saturated Fat 19g, Fiber 2g, Sodium 405mg

Citrusy Beef

PREPARATION TIME: 15 minutes **COOKING TIME:** 75 minutes **SERVES:** 6

INGREDIENTS:

Juice of 1 Lemon

Juice of 2 Oranges

2 pounds Beef, cut into chunks

1 tbsp Ghee

1 tbsp Seasoning by choice

½ tsp Sea Salt

INSTRUCTIONS:

Place the beef in the Instant Pot and sprinkle with salt, pepper, and seasoning. Massage the meat with your hands to season it well. Pour the lemon and orange juice over and then put the lid on. Seal it. Select "MANUAL" and set the cooking time to 50 minutes. Cook on HIGH pressure.

When the timer goes off, turn the pressure handle to "Venting" for a quick pressure release and open the lid carefully. Shred the meat inside the pot with two forks. Keep the lid open and set the Instant Pot to SAUTE. Stir to combine and saute for about 20 minutes, or until the liquid is absorbed. Add the ghee, give the mixture a good stir, and cook for additional 5 minutes. Serve and enjoy!

NUTRITION FACTS PER SERVING:

Calories 477, Protein 36g, Total Carbs 8g, Total Fat 35g, Saturated Fat 17g, Fiber 1g, Sodium 300mg

Beef Ragu

PREPARATION TIME: 10 minutes **COOKING TIME:** 45 minutes **SERVES:** 5

INGREDIENTS:

18 ounces Beef

2 Bay Leaves

5 Garlic Cloves, crushed

7 ounces jarred Roasted Red Peppers, chopped

28 ounces canned crushed Tomatoes

1 tbsp chopped Parsley

½ tbsp Olive Oil

1 tsp Sea Salt

½ tsp Black Pepper

INSTRUCTIONS:

Season the beef with salt and pepper. Turn the Instant Pot on and set it to "SAUTE". Add the oil to it and wait until it becomes hot. Place the beef inside and cook until the meat becomes browned on all sides.

Add the rest of the ingredients and give the mixture a good stir to combine. Close the lid and turn clockwise to seal.

Select the "MANUAL" mode. Set the time to 45 minutes. Cook on HIGH pressure. Select "KEEP WARM/CANCEL" after the beeping sound. Wait for the valve to drop on its own for a natural pressure release. Open the lid carefully and serve.

NUTRITION FACTS PER SERVING:

Calories 240, Protein 29g, Total Carbs 15g, Total Fat 8g, Saturated Fat 4g, Fiber 2g, Sodium 410mg

Beef Pot Roast with Carrots

PREPARATION TIME: 10 minutes **COOKING TIME:** 55 minutes **SERVES:** 6

INGREDIENTS:

1 tbsp Italian Seasoning
5 Carrots, peeled and chopped
2 ½ pounds Beef Roast
2 cups Chicken Stock
2 tbsp Coconut Oil

1 Onion, diced
1 tsp minced Garlic
½ tsp Pepper
½ tsp Sea Salt

INSTRUCTIONS:

Turn the Instant Pot on and set it to "SAUTE" and add the coconut oil to it. When melted, add the onions and cook for 4 minutes.

Add garlic and cook for another minute.

Season the beef with pepper and salt and place it on top of the onions and garlic.

Pour the stock over and put the lid on. Turn it clockwise to seal properly and then hit "MANUAL" after the chime.

Set the cooking time to 40 minutes and cook on HIGH pressure.

Press the "KEEP WARM/CANCEL" button after the beep and immediately move the pressure handle to "Venting" for a quick pressure release.

Open the lid gently and stir in the carrots.

Close and seal the lid again and cook on "MANUAL" for 10 more minutes.

Release the pressure quickly once again. Wait a couple of minutes before serving.

Enjoy!

NUTRITION FACTS PER SERVING:

Calories 710, Protein 55g, Total Carbs 15g, Total Fat 52g, Saturated Fat 27g, Fiber 2g, Sodium 600mg

Beef Coconut Curry

INGREDIENTS:

1 Onion, diced

1 cup Coconut Milk

4 Carrots, sliced

4 Potatoes, peeled and chopped

½ cup Beef Broth

1 pound Beef, cubed

2 tsp minced Garlic

2 tbsp Curry Powder

½ tsp Pepper

½ tsp Paprika

½ tsp Sea Salt

½ tsp dried Parsley

2 tbsp Olive Oil

INSTRUCTIONS:

Set your Instant Pot to "SAUTE" and add the olive oil to it. When it becomes hot and sizzling, add the garlic and onions and cook just for 2 minutes.

Stir in the beef and cook until the meat becomes browned.

Add all of the other ingredients to the pot and make sure to stir well to combine. Put the lid on. Make sure to seal properly by turning it clockwise.

Choose the "MANUAL" cooking mode and set the cooking time to 30 minutes. Cook on HIGH pressure.

When the timer goes off, select "KEEP WARM/CANCEL".

Turn the pressure handle from "Sealing: to "Venting" for a quick pressure release.

Open the lid gently, keeping your hands away from the steam.

Ladle into serving bowls immediately.

Enjoy!

NUTRITION FACTS PER SERVING:

Calories 610, Protein 40g, Total Carbs 47.5g, Total Fat 28.5g, Saturated Fat 18g, Fiber 2g, Sodium 410mg

Beef & Tomato Soup

PREPARATION TIME: 10 minutes **COOKING TIME:** 12 minutes **SERVES:** 4

INGREDIENTS:

1 cup diced Onions

1 cup Chicken Broth

1 cup Coconut Milk

1 ½ cups ground Beef

30 ounces Tomatoes, diced

3 tsp minced Garlic

¼ cup chopped Basil

1 tbsp Coconut Oil

INSTRUCTIONS:

Turn the Instant Pot on and set it to "SAUTE". Add in the coconut oil. When melted, add the beef and cook until it becomes browned. Add onions and garlic and saute for 2 minutes.

Meanwhile, blend together the tomatoes and coconut milk in the blender. When the mixture becomes smooth, pour over the beef. Add the rest of the ingredients and stir to combine well. Close the lid and turn clockwise to seal. Select "MANUAL" and set the cooking time to 4 minutes. Cook on HIGH pressure.

Select "KEEP WARM/CANCEL" when the timer goes off. Wait for the valve to drop on its own for a natural pressure release. Open the lid carefully and serve.

NUTRITION FACTS PER SERVING:

Calories 330, Protein 15g, Total Carbs 15.2g, Total Fat 25g, Saturated Fat 14g, Fiber 4g, Sodium 305mg

Herbed Beef & Yams

PREPARATION TIME: 10 minutes **COOKING TIME:** 40 minutes **SERVES:** 6

INGREDIENTS:

1 Onion, diced

2 Yams, peeled and cubed

1 tbsp chopped Basil

1 tbsp chopped Parsley

1 tbsp chopped Coriander

2 pounds Beef, cubed

1 tsp minced Garlic

1 ½ cups Bone Broth

3 tbsp Tomato Paste

1 Bell Pepper, chopped

1 tbsp Olive Oil

INSTRUCTIONS:

Turn the Instant Pot on and set it to "SAUTE". Add the olive oil to it.

When the oil becomes hot and sizzling, add the peppers and onions and cook for about 3 minutes.

Then, stir in the garlic and saute for another minute.

Add the beef and cook until the meat becomes browned on all sides.

Add the rest of the ingredients to the pot and give the mixture a good stir to combine.

Put the lid on and then turn clockwise to seal. After the chime, click on the "MANUAL" button.

Set the cooking time to 30 minutes. Cook on HIGH pressure.

When the timer goes off, select the "KEEP WARM/CANCEL".

Turn the handle from to "Venting" for a quick pressure release and open the lid carefully.

Serve and enjoy!

NUTRITION FACTS PER SERVING:

Calories 390, Protein 43g, Total Carbs 22g, Total Fat 27g, Saturated Fat 16g, Fiber 1.4g, Sodium 320mg

Lamb Habanero Chili

PREPARATION TIME: 15 minutes **COOKING TIME:** 45 minutes **SERVES:** 4

INGREDIENTS:

1 pound Ground Beef
3 Carrots, chopped
3 Celery Stalks, chopped
1 Bell Pepper, chopped
1 Onion, diced
1 Habanero, minced
1 tsp minced Garlic

14 ounces canned diced Tomatoes
1 tbsp Chili Powder
1 tsp Cumin
½ tsp Paprika
½ tsp Sea Salt
½ tsp Pepper
1 tbsp Olive Oil

INSTRUCTIONS:

Turn the Instant Pot on and set it to "SAUTE".

Add the onions and cook for 3 minutes.

Add garlic and cook for one more. Stir in the ground beef and cook it until the meat becomes brown.

Add all of the other ingredients and give the mixture a good stir until well combined. Close the lid and turn clockwise to seal.

Select the "MEAT/STEW" cooking mode.

Set the cooking time to 35 minutes and cook on HIGH pressure.

When the timer goes off, press the "KEEP WARM/CANCEL" button.

Do a natural pressure release by letting the valve drop on its own.

Open the lid carefully and ladle the chili into serving bowls.

Enjoy!

NUTRITION FACTS PER SERVING:

Calories 330, Protein 37g, Total Carbs 20g, Total Fat 12g, Saturated Fat 4.2g, Fiber 2.5g, Sodium 400mg

Lamb Stew with Apricots

PREPARATION TIME: 10 minutes **COOKING TIME:** 30 minutes **SERVES:** 4

INGREDIENTS:

1 pound Lamb, cubed
4 dried Apricots, diced
1 tsp minced Garlic
1 Onion, diced
2 Sweet Potatoes, peeled and chopped
2 Carrots, peeled and chopped
2 ½ cups Chicken Broth
3 cups chopped Kale

28 ounces diced canned Tomatoes
½ tsp Cinnamon
1 tsp Cumin
½ tsp Ginger Powder
¼ tsp Allspice
¼ tsp Pepper
½ tsp Sea Salt
1 tbsp Olive Oil

INSTRUCTIONS:

Turn your Instant Pot on and set it to "SAUTE". Add the olive oil to it. When the oil becomes hot, add the lamb and cook until the meat becomes brown on all sides.

Add onions and cook for 3 more minutes. When softened a bit, stir in the garlic. Saute only for a minute. Stir in all of the remaining ingredients. Stir well to combine and put the lid on. Make sure to turn the lid clockwise to seal the pot well.

When you hear the chime, press the "MANUAL" button. Set the cooking time to 20 minutes and cook on HIGH pressure.

When the timer goes off, press the "KEEP WARM/CANCEL" button. Turn the pressure handle to "Venting" for a quick pressure release and open the lid carefully.

Serve into bowls immediately.

NUTRITION FACTS PER SERVING:

Calories 420, Protein 43g, Total Carbs 14.2g, Total Fat 18g, Saturated Fat 7.5g, Fiber 2g, Sodium 465mg

Mutton with Potatoes and Tomatoes

INGREDIENTS:

1 pound Mutton, cubed
3 Potatoes, peeled and chopped
1 cup chopped Carrots
½ cup chopped Turnips
2 cups canned diced Tomatoes
1 Onion, diced

2 Garlic Cloves, minced
½ cup Chicken Broth
½ tsp Salt
¼ tsp Black Pepper
1 tbsp Coconut Oil

INSTRUCTIONS:

Turn the Instant Pot on, set it to "SAUTE", and add the coconut oil to it.

When melted, add the mutton pieces and cook them until they become browned on all sides. Transfer to a plate.

Add the onions to the pot and cook them until they become softened, for about 3 minutes. Stir in the garlic and cook just for a minute.

Return the cooked mutton to the pot and add all of the remaining ingredients. Stir well to combine and then put the lid on.

Turn the lid clockwise to seal it properly. After the chiming sound, select the "MANUAL" cooking mode. With the "+" and "-" buttons, set the cooking time to 25 minutes. Cook on HIGH pressure.

When the timer goes off, select "KEEP WARM/CANCEL" to turn the Instant Pot off. Wait for the valve to drop on its own for a natural pressure release.

Open the lid carefully and divide between 4 serving bowls/plates.

Enjoy!

NUTRITION FACTS PER SERVING:

Calories 389, Protein 32g, Total Carbs 37g, Total Fat 13g, Saturated Fat 6.8g, Fiber 6.7g, Sodium 800mg

FISH AND SEAFOOD RECIPES

Tilapia Chowder

PREPARATION TIME: 10 minutes **COOKING TIME:** 15 minutes **SERVES:** 4

INGREDIENTS:

1 ⅓ cups Water
1 cup Almond Milk
1 cup peeled and chopped Potatoes
⅔ pounds Tilapia, chopped
½ cups chopped Celery
⅔ cup Chicken Stock

¾ cup diced Onion
¼ tsp Salt
¼ tsp Pepper
¼ tsp Onion Powder
1 tbsp Arrowroot mixed with 1 ½ tbsp Water

INSTRUCTIONS:

Combine everything except for the arrowroot mixture in your Instant Pot.

Close the lid and turn clockwise to seal.

Select "MANUAL" and set the cooking time to 10 minutes. Cook on HIGH pressure.

When the timer goes off, press the "KEEP WARM/CANCEL" button.

Do a quick pressure release by turning the pressure handle to "Venting". Be sure to keep your hands away from the steam.

Set the Instant Pot to "SAUTE".

Stir in the arrowroot mixture and cook for about 5 minutes, or until the chowder is thickened.

Serve immediately and enjoy!

NUTRITION FACTS PER SERVING:

Calories 320, Protein 25g, Total Carbs 13.5g, Total Fat 16g, Saturated Fat 4g, Fiber 3.2g, Sodium 410mg

Salmon with Broccoli and Potatoes

PREPARATION TIME: 3 minutes **COOKING TIME:** 5 minutes **SERVES:** 1

INGREDIENTS:

4-ounce Salmon Fillet

4 New Potatoes

4 ounces Broccoli Florets

2 tsp Olive Oil

Salt and Pepper, to taste

1 ½ cups Water

INSTRUCTIONS:

Pour the water into your Instant Pot and lower the rack.

Season the potatoes with some salt and pepper and place them on top of the rack. Drizzle half of the oil over.

Close the lid and turn clockwise to seal. Select the "MANUAL" cooking mode and then the cooking time to 2 minutes. Cook on HIGH pressure.

When the timer goes off, press "KEEP WARM/CANCEL" to turn the Instant Pot off.

Move the handle to "Venting" to release the pressure quickly before opening the lid.

Season the broccoli and salmon with salt and pepper, as well.

Arrange the broccoli on top of the potatoes and top with the salmon fillet.

Drizzle them with the remaining olive oil.

Close and seal the lid again and cook on "MANUAL" for 3 more minutes.

Again, do a quick pressure release.

Serve and enjoy!

NUTRITION FACTS PER SERVING:

Calories 440, Protein 35g, Total Carbs 19.5g, Total Fat 15g, Saturated Fat 3.5g, Fiber 4g, Sodium 450mg

Veggie Noodle Salmon

INGREDIENTS:

4 Salmon Fillets
2 tsp Olive Oil
1 large Carrot, peeled and spiralized
2 Large Potatoes, peeled and spiralized

1 Zucchini, peeled and spiralized
1 cup Water
1 Thyme Sprig
¼ tsp Pepper
¼ tsp Salt

INSTRUCTIONS:

Pour the water into your Instant Pot and add the thyme sprig inside.

Arrange the noodles inside the steaming basket and top with the salmon.

Season with salt and pepper and drizzle with the oil.

Place the basket inside the Instant Pot. Close the lid and turn clockwise to seal.

Select the "STEAM" cooking mode.

Set the cooking time to 5 minutes. Cook on HIGH pressure.

When you hear the beep, press the "KEEP WARM/CANCEL" button.

Move the pressure handle from "Sealing" to "Venting" for a quick pressure release and open the lid carefully.

Remove the steaming basket from the Instant Pot gently, and serve the veggies and salmon.

Enjoy!

NUTRITION FACTS PER SERVING:

Calories 310, Protein 40g, Total Carbs 12g, Total Fat 13g, Saturated Fat 4g, Fiber 3.5g, Sodium 350mg

Sea Bass Stew

PREPARATION TIME: 10 minutes **COOKING TIME:** 15 minutes **SERVES:** 4

INGREDIENTS:

1 Red Onion, diced

4 tbsp Olive Oil

½ cup Chicken Broth

1 cup Clam Juice

½ pound Potatoes, peeled and cubed

2 ½ cups Water

14 ounces canned diced Tomatoes

1 ½ pounds Sea Bass Fillets, chopped

1 tsp minced Garlic

2 tbsp chopped Dill

2 tbsp Lemon Juice

Salt and Pepper, to taste

INSTRUCTIONS:

Turn the Instant Pot on and set it to "SAUTE".

Add half of the oil and heat it until sizzling. When hot enough, add the onions and cook for 3 minutes. Add the garlic and saute for a minute. Pour the broth over and deglaze the bottom of the pot. Stir in the tomatoes, potatoes, water, and clam juice.

Close the lid and turn clockwise to seal. Select the "MANUAL" cooking mode. Set the cooking time to 5 minutes. Cook on HIGH pressure.

When the timer goes off, hit "KEEP WARM/CANCEL" to turn the Instant Pot off. Move the pressure handle to "Venting" to do a quick pressure release. Open the lid carefully and add the sea bass pieces.

Close and seal the lid again and cook on "MANUAL" for another 5 minutes. Again, turn the Instant Pot off, do a quick pressure release, and open the lid. Press the "SAUTE" button.

Stir in the remaining ingredients (along with the rest of the oil), and cook for 3 more minutes with the lid off. Ladle into serving bowls immediately.

Enjoy!

NUTRITION FACTS PER SERVING:

Calories 390, Protein 37g, Total Carbs 17g, Total Fat 18g, Saturated Fat 5.5g, Fiber 3.5g, Sodium 490mg

Crab Cakes

PREPARATION TIME: 10 minutes **COOKING TIME:** 4 minutes **SERVES:** 2

INGREDIENTS:

1 cup Crab Meat
¼ cup chopped Black Olives
1 Carrot, shredded
½ cup boiled and mashed Potatoes
¼ cup Almond Flour

¼ cup grated Onion
1 ½ cup canned diced Tomatoes
1 tbsp Olive Oil
¼ cup Chicken Broth

INSTRUCTIONS:

Place the crab meat, carrots, olives, flour, potatoes, and onion, in a bowl. Mix with your hands until the mixture is fully incorporated.

Shape the mixture into two patties.

Add the olive oil to the Instant Pot and set it to "SAUTE".

When hot and sizzling, add the crab cakes and cook for a minute.

Flip them over and cook for another minute.

Pour the tomatoes and broth over and close the lid. Turn it clockwise to seal properly.

Select the "MANUAL" cooking mode and set the cooking time to 2 minutes. Cook on HIGH pressure.

When the timer goes off, select "KEEP WARM/CANCEL".

Turn the pressure handle to "Venting" for a quick pressure release and open the lid carefully.

Serve and enjoy!

NUTRITION FACTS PER SERVING:

Calories 300, Protein 19g, Total Carbs 11g, Total Fat 8g, Saturated Fat 1.5g, Fiber 1g, Sodium 150mg

VEGAN AND VEGETARIAN RECIPES

Potato Chili

PREPARATION TIME: 10 minutes **COOKING TIME:** 12 minutes **SERVES:** 4

INGREDIENTS:

4 cups Vegetable Broth
3 large Russet Potatoes, peeled and diced
2 Jalapeno Peppers, seeded and diced
1 Garlic Clove, minced

½ tsp Cumin
1 tsp Chili Powder
¼ tsp Cayenne Pepper
½ Red Onion, diced
1 tbsp Olive Oil

INSTRUCTIONS:

Add the olive oil to the Instant Pot and set it to "SAUTE". When hot and sizzling add the onions and cook for 2-3 minutes.

When translucent, add the garlic and cook for another minute.

Add the remaining ingredients and stir well to combine.

Put the lid on and turn it clockwise to seal. Select "MANUAL" and set the cooking time to 8 minutes. Cook on HIGH.

After the beeping sound, hit "KEEP WARM/CANCEL" to turn the Instant Pot off.

Let the pressure release naturally, by allowing the valve to drop on its own.

Open the lid carefully.

Serve and enjoy!

NUTRITION FACTS PER SERVING:

Calories 255, Protein 6g, Total Carbs 50g, Total Fat 5g, Saturated Fat 1.5g, Fiber 4g, Sodium 320mg

Potato and Spinach Bowl

PREPARATION TIME: 10 minutes **COOKING TIME:** 5 minutes **SERVES:** 4

INGREDIENTS:

1 Sweet Potato, peeled and cubed
1 Onion, chopped
2 cups Spinach
2 Garlic Cloves, minced
½ cup Veggie Broth

1 tsp Lemon Juice
1 tsp ground Ginger
½ tsp Cayenne Pepper
½ tbsp Olive Oil
¼ tsp Pepper

INSTRUCTIONS:

Turn your Instant Pot on and press the "SAUTE" button.

Add the olive oil to it.

When hot and sizzling, add the onion and cook for 2 minutes.

Add the garlic, ginger, cayenne, and pepper, and cook for one more minute.

Add the sweet potatoes and cook for another minute.

Pour the broth over and stir in the spinach.

Close the lid and turn it clockwise to seal.

Select "MANUAL" and set the cooking time to 4 minutes. Cook on HIGH.

After the beeping sound, press the "KEEP WARM/CANCEL" button.

Move the pressure handle to "Venting" to release the pressure quickly.

Open the lid carefully.

Serve and enjoy!

NUTRITION FACTS PER SERVING:

Calories 150, Protein 4g, Total Carbs 14g, Total Fat 5g, Saturated Fat 2g, Fiber 2.3g, Sodium 345mg

Root Veggie Casserole

PREPARATION TIME: 10 minutes **COOKING TIME:** 16 minutes **SERVES:** 4

INGREDIENTS:

1 Onion, diced	1 tsp Thyme
4 pounds Baby Potatoes, halved	1 tsp dried Parsley
2 pounds Baby Carrots	2 tbsp Olive Oil
1 tsp minced Garlic	½ cup Veggie Broth

INSTRUCTIONS:

Add the olive oil to the Instant Pot and set it to "SAUTE". When hot and sizzling add the onions and cook for 2-3 minutes. When the onions become translucent, add the garlic and cook for another minute. Add the carrots and cook for another 3 minutes. Stir in the rest of the ingredients and put the lid on. Seal by turning clockwise and then press "MANUAL". Set the cooking time to 10 minutes and cook on HIGH.

After the beeping sound, hit "KEEP WARM/CANCEL" to turn the Instant Pot off. Release the pressure quickly by moving the handle from "Sealing" to "Venting". Open the lid carefully. Serve and enjoy!

NUTRITION FACTS PER SERVING:

Calories 330, Protein 7g, Total Carbs 65g, Total Fat 5g, Saturated Fat 2g, Fiber 8g, Sodium 422mg

Coconut and Zucchini Soup

PREPARATION TIME: 10 minutes **COOKING TIME:** 10 minutes **SERVES:** 10

INGREDIENTS:

32 ounces Veggie Broth	1 tbsp Curry Paste
10 cups chopped Zucchini	½ tsp Garlic Powder
13 ounces Coconut Milk	½ tsp Onion Powder

INSTRUCTIONS:

Place all of the ingredients in the Instant Pot. Give the mixture a good stir to combine and then put the lid on. Turn it clockwise to seal. After you hear the chime, select "MANUAL" and set the cooking time to 10 minutes. Cook on HIGH.

When the timer goes off, turn the Instant Pot off by pressing "KEEP WARM/ CANCEL". Do a quick pressure release by moving the pressure handle to "Venting". Be careful not to burn yourself and open the lid slowly. Serve immediately and enjoy!

NUTRITION FACTS PER SERVING:

Calories 110, Protein 3g, Total Carbs 6g, Total Fat 10g, Saturated Fat 5.6g, Fiber 1g, Sodium 210mg

Lime & Mint Zoodles

PREPARATION TIME: 5 minutes **COOKING TIME:** 3 minutes **SERVES:** 2

INGREDIENTS:

2 Zucchini, spiralized
1 tsp Lime Zest
2 tbsp Lime Juice
2 tbsp chopped Mint

1 tbsp Coconut Oil
2 tbsp Olive Oil
1 tsp minced Garlic
¼ tsp Black Pepper

INSTRUCTIONS:

Add the olive oil to the Instant Pot and set it to "SAUTE". When hot and sizzling add the garlic and the lime zest and cook for about 30 seconds. Add the rest of the ingredients, stir well to combine, and cook for only 2 minutes.

Divide the mixture among two serving bowls. Enjoy!

NUTRITION FACTS PER SERVING:

Calories 180, Protein 4g, Total Carbs 12g, Total Fat 15g, Saturated Fat 4g, Fiber 1g, Sodium 200mg

Walnut & Cinnamon Sweet Potatoes

PREPARATION TIME: 10 minutes **COOKING TIME:** 7 minutes **SERVES:** 4

INGREDIENTS:

4 Sweet Potatoes, boiled and mashed
2 tbsp Coconut Flour
¼ tsp Cinnamon
2 tbsp Coconut Milk
½ cup chopped Walnuts
1 tbsp Coconut Oil
2 tbsp Fresh Orange Juice
1 cup Water

INSTRUCTIONS:

Add the mashed potatoes, coconut milk, cinnamon, orange juice, and coconut oil, to a large bowl. Mix well until the mixture is fully incorporated. Grease a baking dish with some cooking spray and then press the potato mixture at the bottom well. Top with the walnuts and sprinkle the coconut flour over.

Pour the water into the Instant Pot and lower the trivet. Place the baking dish on top of the trivet. Put the lid on and seal it by turning clockwise. Select "MANUAL" and set the cooking time to 7 minutes. Cook on HIGH.

After you hear the beep, press the "KEEP WARM/CANCEL" button to turn the Instant Pot off. Let the pressure release naturally, by allowing the valve to drop on its own. Open the lid carefully. Serve and enjoy!

NUTRITION FACTS PER SERVING:

Calories 400, Protein 5g, Total Carbs 67g, Total Fat 15g, Saturated Fat 10g, Fiber 8g, Sodium 410mg

Zucchini Coconut Burgers

PREPARATION TIME: 10 minutes **COOKING TIME:** 6 minutes **SERVES:** 4

INGREDIENTS:

¼ cup Coconut Flakes, unsweetened
¼ cup Coconut Flour
½ cup Mashed Potatoes
1 large Zucchini, shredded
2 tbsp Olive Oil

INSTRUCTIONS:

Add the olive oil to your Instant Pot and heat it on "SAUTE".

Place all of the remaining ingredients in a bowl. Mix with your hands until fully incorporated and then shape the mixture into 4 equal patties. When the oil becomes hot and sizzling, add the patties and cook them for 3 minutes per side. Serve.

NUTRITION FACTS PER SERVING:

Calories 300, Protein 5g, Total Carbs 13g, Total Fat 5g, Saturated Fat 1g, Fiber 2g, Sodium 320g

Cauliflower Tabbouleh with Mint and Parsley

PREPARATION TIME: 5 minutes **COOKING TIME:** 3 minutes **SERVES:** 3

INGREDIENTS:

2 cups Cauliflower Rice
4 tbsp Olive Oil
⅓ cup chopped Spring Onions
½ Cucumber, diced
3 tbsp Lime Juice

½ cup Parsley
½ cup Mint
1 tsp minced Garlic
1 cup diced Tomatoes

INSTRUCTIONS:

Add a tablespoon of the olive oil to the Instant Pot and set it to "SAUTE". When hot, add the garlic and cook for a minute. Add the tomatoes and cauliflower and saute them for about 2-3 minutes. Transfer to a bowl.

Add the remaining ingredients to the bowl and give the mixture a good stir to combine well. Divide among 3 serving bowls. Enjoy!

NUTRITION FACTS PER SERVING:

Calories 220, Protein 2g, Total Carbs 4g, Total Fat 18g, Saturated Fat 8g, Fiber 3g, Sodium 205mg

Potato & Leek Patties

PREPARATION TIME: 10 minutes **COOKING TIME:** 6 minutes **SERVES:** 3

INGREDIENTS:

1 tbsp Olive Oil

4 ounces Leek, sliced

9 ounces Potatoes, boiled and mashed

⅓ cup Almond Flour

1 tbsp Coconut Cream

¼ tsp Onion Powder

¼ tsp Paprika

¼ tsp Garlic Powder

Pinch of Pepper

INSTRUCTIONS:

You will not be pressure cooking these patties so you don't need any water.

Place all of the ingredients, except the oil, in a bowl. Mix with your hands until well combined and shape the mixture into 3 large or 6 small patties.

Add the olive oil to the Instant Pot and set it to "SAUTE". When hot, add the patties and cook them for about 3 minutes on each side. Serve as desired.

NUTRITION FACTS PER SERVING:

Calories 260, Protein 10g, Total Carbs 30g, Total Fat 11g, Saturated Fat 4.8g, Fiber 4g, Sodium 450mg

Cabbage, Beet & Apple Stew

PREPARATION TIME: 10 minutes **COOKING TIME:** 20 minutes **SERVES:** 4

INGREDIENTS:

2 Carrots, chopped

½ Cabbage, chopped

1 Apple, diced

1 Onion, diced

1 tbsp grated Ginger

2 Beets, chopped

4 cups Veggie Broth

2 tbsp chopped Parsley

½ tsp Garlic Salt

¼ tsp Pepper

INSTRUCTIONS:

Place all of the ingredients in your Instant Pot. Stir well to combine everything and close the lid. Turn it clockwise to seal and then hit the "MANUAL" button. Set the cooking time to 20 minutes and cook on HIGH pressure.

After you hear the beep, select "KEEP WARM/CANCEL". Move the pressure handle from "Sealing" to "Venting" for a quick pressure release and open the lid carefully. Pour into serving bowls and serve immediately. Enjoy!

NUTRITION FACTS PER SERVING:

Calories 135, Protein 7.5g, Total Carbs 24g, Total Fat 2g, Saturated Fat 1g, Fiber 5g, Sodium 820mg

Basil and Tomato "Pasta"

PREPARATION TIME: 10 minutes **COOKING TIME:** 2 minutes **SERVES:** 4

INGREDIENTS:

½ cup Tomato Paste
4 cups Zoodles (spiralized Zucchini)
¼ cup Coconut Cream
2 Garlic Cloves, minced
¼ cup Veggie Broth
2 cups canned diced Tomatoes
2 tbsp chopped Basil
1 tsp chopped Parsley

INSTRUCTIONS:

Place all of the ingredients in your Instant Pot. Stir well to combine everything. Put the lid on and turn it clockwise to seal. Select "MANUAL" after you hear the sealing chime and then set the cooking time to 2 minutes. Cook on HIGH.

When the timer goes off, hit "KEEP WARM/CANCEL" to turn the Instant Pot off. Move the handle from "Sealing" to "Venting" for a quick pressure release. Open the lid carefully. Serve and enjoy!

NUTRITION FACTS PER SERVING:

Calories 70, Protein 2g, Total Carbs 10g, Total Fat 4g, Saturated Fat 1.5g, Fiber 2.5g, Sodium 200mg

Squash and Sweet Potato Lunch Soup

PREPARATION TIME: 15 minutes **COOKING TIME:** 15 minutes **SERVES:** 4

INGREDIENTS:

2 cups cubed Squash
2 cups cubed Sweet Potatoes
2 tbsp Coconut Oil
1 Onion, diced

1 tbsp Coconut Cream
3 cups Veggie Broth
Pinch of Thyme

INSTRUCTIONS:

Turn the Instant Pot on and press the "SAUTE" button. Melt the coconut oil. Add the onion and cook until they become soft, 3 minutes. Stir in the potatoes and squash and cook for an additional minute, or until they begin to 'sweat'. Pour the broth over and stir in the thyme. Close the lid and turn it clockwise. When sealed, choose "MANUAL" and set the time to 10 minutes. Cook on HIGH.

Select "KEEP WARM/CANCEL" after the beep. Allow the valve to drop on its own for a natural pressure release. Open the lid carefully and stir in the coconut cream. Serve immediately and enjoy!

NUTRITION FACTS PER SERVING:

Calories 240, Protein 6.5g, Total Carbs 35g, Total Fat 9g, Saturated Fat 2g, Fiber 3g, Sodium 240mg

Tomato and Kale "Rice"

PREPARATION TIME: 10 minutes **COOKING TIME:** 5 minutes **SERVES:** 4

INGREDIENTS:

1 tbsp Coconut Oil
⅓ cup Veggie Broth
4 cups Cauliflower Rice
1 Large Tomato, chopped

½ cup chopped Kale
1 tsp chopped Cilantro
¼ tsp Pepper
¼ tsp Garlic Powder

INSTRUCTIONS:

Turn your Instant Pot on and press "SAUTE". Melt coconut oil and cook the tomato, cauliflower, pepper, and garlic powder for a minute. Pour the broth over and stir in the spinach. Close the lid and turn it clockwise to seal properly.

Select "MANUAL" and set the cooking time to 3 minutes on HIGH. After you hear the beep, move the pressure handle from "Sealing" to "Venting" to release the pressure quickly. Open the lid carefully. Serve and enjoy!

NUTRITION FACTS PER SERVING:

Calories 180, Protein 4g, Total Carbs 4.8g, Total Fat 3g, Saturated Fat 1g, Fiber 1.3g, Sodium 180mg

Beet Borscht

PREPARATION TIME: 10 minutes **COOKING TIME:** 52 minutes **SERVES:** 8

INGREDIENTS:

3 cups shredded Cabbage   3 cups Veggie Stock
8 cups diced Beets   2 Carrots, diced
3 Celery Stalks, diced   1 tsp Thyme
1 Onion, diced   ¼ tsp Pepper
1 Garlic Clove, diced   1 ½ cups Water

INSTRUCTIONS:

Pour the water into the Instant Pot and lower a steamer basket. Place in the beets and seal the lid. Select "MANUAL". Set to 7 minutes. Cook on HIGH.

After the beeping sound, release the pressure quickly. Remove the steamer basket water. Return the beets to the pot and add the rest of the ingredients. Seal the lid again. Select "SOUP" and cook for 45 minutes. When the timer goes off, let the valve drop on its own for a natural pressure release. Serve and enjoy!

NUTRITION FACTS PER SERVING:

Calories 110, Protein 4g, Total Carbs 24g, Total Fat 2g, Saturated Fat 1g, Fiber 5g, Sodium 385mg

Veggie Flax Burgers

PREPARATION TIME: 20 minutes **COOKING TIME:** 11 minutes **SERVES:** 4

INGREDIENTS:

2 tbsp Olive Oil

1 bag of Frozen Mixed Veggies
(broccoli, carrots, peas, etc.)

1 cup Cauliflower Florets

1 cup Flax Meal

1 ½ cups Water

INSTRUCTIONS:

Pour the water into your Instant Pot. Combine the mixed veggies and cauliflower florets in the steaming basket and then lower the basket into the pot. Close the lid and turn clockwise to seal. Choose "MANUAL" and set the cooking time to 4 or 5 minutes. Cook on HIGH.

Press the "KEEP WARM/CANCEL" button after the timer goes off. Move the pressure handle from "Sealing" to "Venting" for a quick pressure release and open the lid carefully. Transfer the veggies to a bowl and discard the water.

Mash the veggies with a potato masher and allow them to cool a bit, about 10 minutes. When safe to handle, stir in the flax meal and shape the mixture into 4 equal patties.

Wipe the Instant Pot clean and add the olive oil to it. Set it to "SAUTE" and wait until the oil becomes hot. When sizzling, add the veggie burgers. Cook for 3 minutes then flip over and cook for additional 3 minutes on the other side. Serve.

NUTRITION FACTS PER SERVING:

Calories 220, Protein 4g, Total Carbs 7.5g, Total Fat 10g, Saturated Fat 4g, Fiber 3g, Sodium 365mg

VEGETABLES AND SIDE DISHES

Classic Mashed Potatoes

PREPARATION TIME: 10 minutes **COOKING TIME:** 8 minutes **SERVES:** 4

INGREDIENTS:

4 Medium Potatoes

2 tbsp Coconut Oil

¼ cup Coconut Milk

Pinch of Nutmeg

Pinch of Sea Salt

Pinch of Black Pepper

Water, as needed

INSTRUCTIONS:

Wash and peel the potatoes. Place them inside the Instant Pot, whole.

Add water, just enough to cover the potatoes. Put the lid of the Instant Pot on and then it clockwise for a proper sealing.

When you hear the chime, hit "MANUAL". Set the cooking time to 8 minutes and cook on HIGH pressure.

Once you hear the beep, press the "KEEP WARM/CANCEL" button.

Turn the pressure handle to "Venting" to release the pressure quickly and open the lid carefully.

Transfer the potatoes to a bowl. Grab a potato masher and mash the cooked potatoes well until there are no more lumps left.

Stir in the remaining ingredients until the mixture is well-combined and smooth.

Serve and enjoy!

NUTRITION FACTS PER SERVING:

Calories 210, Protein 4g, Total Carbs 34g, Total Fat 7g, Saturated Fat 2.5g, Fiber 5g, Sodium 450mg

Garlic & Herb Potatoes

PREPARATION TIME: 10 minutes **COOKING TIME:** 6 minutes **SERVES:** 2

INGREDIENTS:

1 pound Potatoes, peeled and quartered
1 tbsp chopped Cilantro
1 tbsp chopped Parsley

1 tbsp chopped Basil
3 tsp minced Garlic
3 tbsp Coconut Oil, melted
1 cup Water

INSTRUCTIONS:

Pour the water into the Instant Pot and lower the trivet.

Place the potatoes in a baking dish that fits into the Instant Pot.

Sprinkle the herbs and garlic over and drizzle with the melted coconut oil.

Place the baking dish on top of the trivet and then put the lid of the Instant Pot on.

To seal the Instant Pot, turn the lid clockwise. You should hear a chiming sound. After that, select the "MANUAL" cooking mode.

Set the cooking time to 6 minutes and cook on HIGH pressure.

After the beep, select the "KEEP WARM/CANCEL" button to turn the Instant Pot off.

Turn the pressure handle to "Venting" to release the pressure quickly.

Open the lid carefully and take the dish out of the Instant Pot.

Serve and enjoy!

NUTRITION FACTS PER SERVING:

Calories 320, Protein 6g, Total Carbs 43g, Total Fat 15g, Saturated Fat 6.5g, Fiber 4g, Sodium 350mg

Lime Cabbage with Coconut

PREPARATION TIME: 10 minutes **COOKING TIME:** 10 minutes **SERVES:** 4

INGREDIENTS:

1 tbsp Coconut Oil
½ cup desiccated Coconut
⅓ cup Lime Juice
1 Cabbage, shredded
1 Onion, sliced

1 Carrot, sliced
1 tsp minced Garlic
½ tsp Curry Powder
¼ tsp Turmeric Powder

INSTRUCTIONS:

Turn the Instant Pot on, set it to "SAUTE", and add the coconut oil to it.

When melted, add the onion slices and cook them for about 3-4 minutes.

When softened, add the garlic and saute for another minute.

Add the rest of the ingredients to the pot and stir well until everything is well combined.

Close the lid and turn clockwise to seal. Press "MANUAL" after the chime.

Set the cooking time to 5 minutes with the "+" and "-" buttons. Cook on HIGH pressure.

Turn the Instant Pot off by pressing the "KEEP WARM/CANCEL" button after the beep.

Turn the handle from "Sealing" to "Venting" for a quick pressure release and open the lid carefully.

Serve immediately and enjoy!

NUTRITION FACTS PER SERVING:

Calories 190, Protein 4.5g, Total Carbs 20g, Total Fat 11g, Saturated Fat 4.3g, Fiber 5g, Sodium 320mg

Turmeric Carrot Mash

PREPARATION TIME: 10 minutes **COOKING TIME:** 4 minutes **SERVES:** 4

INGREDIENTS:

1 tsp Turmeric Powder

¼ tsp Black Pepper

¼ tsp Sea Salt

1 ½ pounds Carrots, chopped

1 tbsp Coconut Cream

1 ½ cups Water

INSTRUCTIONS:

Pour the water into the Instant Pot.

Place the carrot inside the steaming basket then lower the basket into the pot.

Close the lid of the Instant Pot. To seal, turn the lid clockwise.

Select the "MANUAL" cooking mode after the chime. Using the "+" and "-" buttons, set the time to 4 minutes. Make sure to cook on HIGH pressure.

When the timer goes off, press the "KEEP WARM/CANCEL" button.

Turn the pressure handle to "Venting" to release the pressure quickly.

Open the lid carefully, keeping your hands away from the steam.

Take out the steaming basket and transfer the carrots to a food processor.

Add the rest of the ingredients.

Process until smooth.

Serve and enjoy!

NUTRITION FACTS PER SERVING:

Calories 45, Protein 11g, Total Carbs 11g, Total Fat 1g, Saturated Fat 0g, Fiber 1g, Sodium 320mg

Simple Steamed Potatoes

PREPARATION TIME: 7 minutes **COOKING TIME:** 8 minutes **SERVES:** 8

INGREDIENTS:

3 pounds Potatoes, peeled and quartered

1 tsp Cayenne Pepper

1 tsp Sea Salt

½ tsp Black Pepper

Water, as needed

INSTRUCTIONS:

Place the potatoes inside the Instant Pot.

Add enough water to cover them.

Close the lid and turn clockwise to seal.

Choose the "MANUAL" mode and then set the cooking time to 8 minutes.

Cook on HIGH pressure.

When the timer goes off, press the "KEEP WARM/CANCEL" button.

Turn the pressure handle to "Venting" to do a quick pressure release.

Drain the potatoes and place them in a bowl.

Chop them if you want to.

Sprinkle with the seasonings and serve.

Enjoy!

NUTRITION FACTS PER SERVING:

Calories 190, Protein 3g, Total Carbs 27g, Total Fat 1g, Saturated Fat 0g, Fiber 3g, Sodium 440mg

Creamy Potato and Scallion Salad

PREPARATION TIME: 15 minutes **COOKING TIME:** 10 minutes **SERVES:** 6

INGREDIENTS:

½ cup chopped Scallions
3 Celery Stalks, chopped
1 Large Carrot, peeled and chopped
½ Red Onion, sliced
4 Hardboiled Eggs, sliced, optional
1 ½ pounds Potatoes
⅓ cup Mayonnaise(or Avocado Oil

Mayo)
1/2 tbsp Vinegar
½ tsp Sea Salt
⅓ tsp Cayenne Pepper
¼ tsp Black Pepper
2 cups Water

INSTRUCTIONS:

Wash the potatoes well, scrub them, and place inside the Instant Pot. Pour the water over them and put the lid on. Turn it clockwise to seal.

Select the "MANUAL" cooking mode. Set the cooking time to 10 minutes. Cook on HIGH pressure.

When the timer goes off, turn the Instant Pot off by selecting "KEEP WARM/ CANCEL". Turn the handle to "Venting" for a quick pressure release and open the lid carefully. Transfer the potatoes to a bowl and let them cool slightly.

When safe to handle, peel the potatoes and chop them. Season the potatoes with salt, cayenne, and black pepper.

Place the potatoes in a bowl along with the carrot, celery, onion, and scallions. In a small bowl, whisk together the mayo and vinegar and sprinkle over the salad. If using eggs, slice them thinly and arrange on top.

Serve and enjoy!

NUTRITION FACTS PER SERVING:

Calories 225, Protein 7g, Total Carbs 39.5g, Total Fat 8g, Saturated Fat 3.5g, Fiber 5g, Sodium 510mg

Cabbage, Pear, and Onion Side

PREPARATION TIME: 10 minutes **COOKING TIME:** 25 minutes **SERVES:** 4

INGREDIENTS:

1 pound Cabbage, shredded
1 cup diced Onions
1 cup peeled and chopped Pears
1 tbsp Arrowroot
2 tbsp Water

1 ½ cups Chicken or Veggie Stock
1 tbsp Coconut Oil
½ tsp Sea Salt
¼ tsp Pepper
¼ tsp Cumin

INSTRUCTIONS:

Turn the Instant Pot on. Set it to "SAUTE" and add the coconut oil to it.

When melted, add the onions and pears and cook for about 6-7 minutes.

When softened, add the rest of the ingredients except the arrowroot and water.

Close the lid and turn clockwise to seal. Select the "MANUAL" cooking mode. Set the cooking time to 15 minutes. Cook on HIGH pressure.

When the timer goes off, press the "KEEP WARM/CANCEL" button.

Turn the handle to "Venting" for a quick pressure release, then open the lid carefully. Whisk together the arrowroot and water and then whisk this mixture into the pot.

Set the Instant Pot to "SAUTE" again.

Cook until the sauce thickens, about 3 minutes.

Serve and enjoy!

NUTRITION FACTS PER SERVING:

Calories 160, Protein 3g, Total Carbs 24g, Total Fat 5g, Saturated Fat 1.5g, Fiber 5g, Sodium 450mg

Cauliflower and Pea Bowl

PREPARATION TIME: 10 minutes **COOKING TIME:** 20 minutes **SERVES:** 8

INGREDIENTS:

6 cups Cauliflower Florets

2 Sweet Potatoes, peeled and cubed

2 Tomatoes, diced

2 cups Peas

1 tsp minced Garlic

1 cup chopped Scallions

1 tbsp Coconut Oil

4 cups Stock, Veggie or Chicken

Salt and Pepper, to taste

INSTRUCTIONS:

Turn the Instant Pot on and set it to "SAUTE".

Add the coconut oil to it. When the oil becomes melted, add the scallions. Cook for about 3-4 minutes.

Then, add the cauliflower, tomatoes, and stock.

Close the lid and turn clockwise to seal. Select the "MANUAL" cooking mode and set the cooking time to 6 minutes. Cook on HIGH pressure.

After the beep, press the "KEEP WARM/CANCEL" button.

Turn the pressure handle to "Venting" for a quick pressure release and open the lid carefully. Stir in the remaining ingredients.

Close and seal the lid and hit "MANUAL" once again.

Cook for 10 more minutes. Do a quick pressure release again.

Open the lid and serve. Enjoy!

NUTRITION FACTS PER SERVING:

Calories 150, Protein 6g, Total Carbs 24g, Total Fat 4g, Saturated Fat 1g, Fiber 5g, Sodium 400mg

Stewed Yams with Zucchini

PREPARATION TIME: 10 minutes **COOKING TIME:** 15 minutes **SERVES:** 4

INGREDIENTS:

1 pound Yams, peeled and diced
2 Zucchinis, peeled and chopped
2 Large Tomatoes, chopped
1 tsp minced Garlic
1 Onion, diced

1 cup Chicken Stock
¼ tsp Cayenne Pepper
1 tsp Italian Seasoning
Salt and Pepper, to taste
1 tbsp Olive Oil

INSTRUCTIONS:

Turn the Instant Pot on and set it to "SAUTE".

Add the olive oil to it and heat until sizzling.

Add the onions and cook for about 4 minutes.

When soft, add the garlic and cook for another minute.

Stir in the remaining ingredients and then put the lid of the Instant Pot on.

Turn it clockwise to seal properly and then select "MANUAL" after you hear the chime.

Set the cooking time to 10 minutes and cook on HIGH pressure.

When the timer goes off, press the "KEEP WARM/CANCEL".

Shift the pressure handle to "Venting" for a quick pressure release.

Open the lid gently, keeping your hands away from the steam.

Serve and enjoy!

NUTRITION FACTS PER SERVING:

Calories 225, Protein 4g, Total Carbs 42g, Total Fat 6g, Saturated Fat 2g, Fiber 3g, Sodium 350mg

Potatoes and Green Beans

PREPARATION TIME: 10 minutes **COOKING TIME:** 12 minutes **SERVES:** 6

INGREDIENTS:

½ pound Green Beans, chopped
1 ½ pound Potatoes, peeled and chopped
1 tsp minced Garlic
1 Onion, diced

½ tsp Turmeric Powder
¼ tsp Hot Paprika
1 tbsp Olive Oil
Salt and Pepper, to taste
Water, as needed

INSTRUCTIONS:

Turn the Instant Pot on and set it to "SAUTE". Heat the olive oil in it.

When hot and sizzling, add the onions and cook them for about 3 minutes.

Once they become softened, add the garlic and saute just for a minute.

Add the potatoes and cover them with water.

Close the lid and turn clockwise to seal. Select the "MANUAL" cooking mode. Set the cooking time to 5 minutes. Cook on HIGH pressure.

Hit "KEEP WARM/CANCEL" after the beep and turn the pressure handle to "Venting" for a quick pressure release.

Open the lid and stir in the green beans. Cover and seal and cook for 3 more minutes on "MANUAL".

Again, release the pressure quickly. Season the potatoes and green beans with turmeric, hot paprika, salt, and pepper.

Serve and enjoy!

NUTRITION FACTS PER SERVING:

Calories 120, Protein 3g, Total Carbs 14g, Total Fat 7g, Saturated Fat 2g, Fiber 3g, Sodium 510mg

Lemony Rutabaga and Green Onion Salad

PREPARATION TIME: 10 minutes **COOKING TIME:** 8 minutes **SERVES:** 4

INGREDIENTS:

1 cup sliced Green Onions
2 Rutabagas, peeled and cubed
1 tbsp Coconut Oil
4 tbsp Olive Oil

2 tbsp Lemon Juice
Salt and Pepper, to taste
1 cup Water

INSTRUCTIONS:

Turn the Instant Pot on and set it to "SAUTE".

Add the coconut oil to it. When melted, add the green onions and cook them for about 2-3 minutes.

Add the rutabaga and pour the water over.

Close the lid and turn clockwise to seal. Select "MANUAL" and set the cooking time to 5 minutes. Cook on HIGH pressure.

When the timer goes off, hit "KEEP WARM/CANCEL" to turn the Instant Pot off.

Turn the pressure handle from "Sealing" to "Venting" to release the pressure quickly.

Open the lid carefully.

Drain the rutabaga and green onions and place them in a bowl.

Mix together the remaining ingredients in another bowl and pour the mixture over the rutabaga.

Serve and enjoy!

NUTRITION FACTS PER SERVING:

Calories 185, Protein 3g, Total Carbs 18g, Total Fat 13g, Saturated Fat 5g, Fiber 3g, Sodium 300mg

Garlicky Sweet Potato Mash

PREPARATION TIME: 10 minutes **COOKING TIME:** 10 minutes **SERVES:** 6

INGREDIENTS:

4 Garlic Cloves, minced
¾ cup Coconut Milk
2 tbsp Coconut Oil
2 pounds Sweet Potatoes, peeled and chopped

½ tsp Sea Salt
¼ tsp Pepper
Pinch of Nutmeg
Pinch of dried Thyme
Water, as needed

INSTRUCTIONS:

Place the sweet potato chunks inside the Instant Pot.

Add enough water to cover the potatoes.

Close the lid and turn it clockwise to seal properly.

Select the "MANUAL" cooking mode and then set the cooking time to 10 minutes. Cook on HIGH pressure.

When the timer goes off, press the "KEEP WARM/CANCEL" button to turn the Instant Pot off.

Turn the pressure handle to "Venting" so you can release the pressure quickly.

Drain the potatoes and place in a bowl.

Add the remaining ingredients and mash everything with a potato masher until smooth and creamy.

Serve and enjoy!

NUTRITION FACTS PER SERVING:

Calories 260, Protein 3.5g, Total Carbs 43g, Total Fat 9g, Saturated Fat 2g, Fiber 3g, Sodium 450mg

Pea and Sweet Potato Bowl

PREPARATION TIME: 6 minutes **COOKING TIME:** 14 minutes **SERVES:** 6

INGREDIENTS:

1 pound Sweet Potatoes, peeled and cubed

¾ pound Frozen Peas

1 tsp minced Ginger

1 tsp minced Garlic

¼ tsp dried Thyme

¼ tsp dried Basil

1 ½ cups Chicken Stock

1 tbsp Coconut Oil

INSTRUCTIONS:

Turn the Instant Pot on and set it to "SAUTE". Add the coconut oil to it and cook until melted.

Add the garlic and ginger and cook just for a minute, Add potatoes and pour the stock over.

Close the lid and turn clockwise to seal.

Select the "MANUAL" mode and with the "+" and "-" buttons, set the cooking time to 10 minutes. Cook on HIGH pressure.

After the beep, press the "KEEP WARM/CANCEL" button to turn the Instant Pot off.

Turn the pressure handle to "Venting" for a quick pressure release and open the lid immediately, but be sure to keep your hands away from the steam.

Stir in the peas and seal the lid again.

Again, cook on "MANUAL" for 4 more minutes. Do a quick pressure release again. Drain the potatoes and peas and transfer to a bowl.

Stir in the basil and thyme. Enjoy!

NUTRITION FACTS PER SERVING:

Calories 155, Protein 4.2g, Total Carbs 29g, Total Fat 3g, Saturated Fat 1g, Fiber 3g, Sodium 320mg

Orange Potatoes with Walnuts

PREPARATION TIME: 10 minutes **COOKING TIME:** 10 minutes **SERVES:** 6

INGREDIENTS:

12 Potatoes, peeled and chopped
¾ cup chopped Walnuts
1 cup Mayonnaise (such as Avocado Oil Mayo)
Juice of 1 Lemon

2 tbsp Olive Oil
¼ tsp Ginger Powder
Salt and Pepper, to taste
2 Oranges, peeled and chopped
Water, as needed

INSTRUCTIONS:

Place the potato chunks inside your Instant Pot and add enough water just to cover them.

Close the lid and turn clockwise to seal.

Select the "MANUAL" cooking mode.

Set the cooking time to 10 minutes. Cook on HIGH pressure.

After you hear the beep, press the "KEEP WARM/CANCEL" button.

Turn the pressure handle to "Venting" to release the pressure quickly.

Open the lid, drain the potatoes, and transfer them to a bowl.

Add the oranges and walnuts.

Whisk the rest of the ingredients in a small bowl and pour over the potatoes.

Serve and enjoy!

NUTRITION FACTS PER SERVING:

Calories 300, Protein 6g, Total Carbs 45g, Total Fat 22g, Saturated Fat 11g, Fiber 4g, Sodium 400mg

Garlicky Zucchini and Carrot Noodles

PREPARATION TIME: 10 minutes **COOKING TIME:** 8 minutes **SERVES:** 4

INGREDIENTS:

4 Large Carrots, spirazlized
2 Large Zucchinis, spiralized
2 tsp minced Garlic
1 tbsp Olive Oil

¼ tsp Onion Powder
¼ tsp Pepper
¼ tsp Sea Salt
½ cup Tomato Sauce

INSTRUCTIONS:

Turn the Instant Pot on and set it to "SAUTE".

Add the olive oil to it. When hot and sizzling, add the garlic and cook just for a minute, until it becomes fragrant.

Add the noodles and season with salt, pepper, and onion powder.

Cook for about 3 minutes.

Stir in the tomato sauce and cook for another 4 minutes or so.

Serve and enjoy!

NUTRITION FACTS PER SERVING:

Calories 150, Protein 4g, Total Carbs 16.5g, Total Fat 7g, Saturated Fat 2g, Fiber 4g, Sodium 400mg

FAST SNACKS AND APPETIZERS

Chili Hash Browns

PREPARATION TIME: 10 minutes **COOKING TIME:** 10 minutes **SERVES:** 4

INGREDIENTS:

1 pound Potatoes, peeled and grated
1 tsp Chili Powder
¼ tsp Smoked Paprika

¼ tsp Black Pepper
½ tsp Sea Salt
1 ½ tbsp Coconut Oil

INSTRUCTIONS:

You will not be bringing the pot to pressure for this recipe, so you do not need any liquid.

Turn the Instant Pot on and set it to "SAUTE".

Add the coconut oil to the pot.

When the oil becomes melted, add the potatoes.

Season well with the spices and stir to combine.

Press them with a spatula and cook for about 5 minutes.

Flip the potatoes over and cook for another 5 minutes.

Divide the chili hash browns between 4 plates.

Enjoy!

NUTRITION FACTS PER SERVING:

Calories 160, Protein 2g, Total Carbs 18g, Total Fat 9.5g, Saturated Fat 4g, Fiber 2.5g, Sodium 400mg

Nutty Carrot Sticks

PREPARATION TIME: 10 minutes **COOKING TIME:** 5 minutes **SERVES:** 8

INGREDIENTS:

¼ cup Olive Oil

3 ½ cups Water

3 pounds Carrots, peeled and cut into matchsticks

¼ cup chopped Nuts by choice

(Walnuts and Pine Nuts are great)

2 tbsp Balsamic Vinegar

1 tbsp Orange Juice

2 tsp Lemon Juice

½ tsp Onion Powder

INSTRUCTIONS:

Combine the water and carrots in your Instant Pot.

Close the lid and turn clockwise to seal. Select the "MANUAL" cooking mode.

Set the cooking time to 5 minutes and cook on HIGH.

When the timer goes off, press the "KEEP WARM/CANCEL" button.

Turn the pressure handle to "Venting" for a quick pressure release and open the lid carefully.

Drain the carrots and place in a bowl.

Whisk together the vinegar, orange juice, lemon juice, onion powder, and olive oil.

Pour the mixture over the carrots and toss to coat well.

Sprinkle the nuts over.

Serve and enjoy!

NUTRITION FACTS PER SERVING:

Calories 160, Protein 2g, Total Carbs 18g, Total Fat 10g, Saturated Fat 2g, Fiber 3g, Sodium 250mg

Paprika Potato Slices

PREPARATION TIME: 10 minutes **COOKING TIME:** 3 minutes **SERVES:** 4

INGREDIENTS:

4 Potatoes, peeled and sliced
½ tsp Smoked Paprika
Salt and Pepper, to taste

1 tbsp Coconut Oil
Water, as needed

INSTRUCTIONS:

Place the potato slices inside the Instant Pot and pour enough water to just cover them.

Close the lid and turn clockwise to seal. Select "MANUAL" and set the cooking time to 2 minutes. Cook on HIGH pressure.

When the timer goes off, press the "KEEP WARM/CANCEL" button.

Turn the pressure handle to "Venting" to release the pressure quickly and then open the lid carefully.

Drain the potatoes and discard the water.

Transfer the potatoes to a bowl. Wipe the Instant Pot clean.

Select the "SAUTE" mode and add the coconut oil to it.

Sprinkle the potatoes with paprika, salt, and pepper, and toss to combine well, but be careful not to break them.

When the oil is melted, add the potato slices to the pot and cook for about a minute per side.

Serve and enjoy!

NUTRITION FACTS PER SERVING:

Calories 185, Protein 3g, Total Carbs 29g, Total Fat 7g, Saturated Fat 2g, Fiber 4.2g, Sodium 250mg

Salty and Peppery Sweet Potato Snack

PREPARATION TIME: 10 minutes **COOKING TIME:** 11 minutes **SERVES:** 6

INGREDIENTS:

2 pounds Sweet Potatoes

1 tsp Sea Salt

1 tsp Pepper

2 tbsp Olive Oil

1 ½ cups Water

INSTRUCTIONS:

Pour the water into the Instant Pot and lower the trivet. Wash and peel the potatoes and place each of them on a piece of aluminum foil.

Sprinkle the potatoes with salt and pepper and drizzle with olive oil.

Wrap them in foil and place the potato wraps on top of the trivet.

Close the lid and turn clockwise to seal. Select the "MANUAL" cooking mode and set the time to 11 minutes. Make sure that you cook on HIGH pressure.

After the beep, press the "KEEP WARM/CANCEL" button.

Turn the pressure handle to "Venting" for a quick pressure release.

Open the lid carefully and place the potatoes on your kitchen counter.

Unwrap them gently, making sure that you keep your hands away from the steam.

Chop or slice them to your liking.

Enjoy!

NUTRITION FACTS PER SERVING:

Calories 200, Protein 2.5g, Total Carbs 42g, Total Fat 5g, Saturated Fat 1g, Fiber 6g, Sodium 300mg

Garlicky Pepper and Tomato Appetizer

PREPARATION TIME: 5 minutes **COOKING TIME:** 10 minutes **SERVES:** 4-6

INGREDIENTS:

1 pounds Bell Peppers, cut into strips
2 Large Tomatoes, chopped
1 cup Tomato Sauce
¼ cup Chicken Broth

1 tbsp minced Garlic
2 tbsp chopped Parsley
1 tbsp Olive Oil
Salt and Pepper

INSTRUCTIONS:

Turn the Instant Pot on and set it to "SAUTE". Add the olive oil to it. When hot and sizzling, add the peppers and cook for 2-3 minutes. Add garlic and saute for another minute. Stir in the remaining ingredients. Close the lid and turn clockwise to seal. Select the "MANUAL" cooking mode. Set the cooking time to 6 minutes. Cook on HIGH pressure.

After the beeping sound, press the "KEEP WARM/CANCEL" button. Turn the pressure handle to "Venting" to do a quick pressure release. Open the lid gently. Serve and enjoy!

NUTRITION FACTS PER SERVING:

Calories 120, Protein 3g, Total Carbs 11.5g, Total Fat 8g, Saturated Fat 3g, Fiber 3.5g, Sodium 320mg

Porcini and Sesame Dip

PREPARATION TIME: 10 minutes **COOKING TIME:** 5 minutes **SERVES:** 12

INGREDIENTS:

2 pounds Porcini Mushrooms, sliced
2 tbsp Sesame Paste
3 tbsp Sesame Seeds
1 tbsp Lemon Juice

2 tsp minced Garlic
1 tbsp Coconut Oil
2 tbsp Olive Oil
1 cup of Water

INSTRUCTIONS:

Turn the Instant Pot on. Add the coconut oil to it and choose the "SAUTE" mode. When melted, add the garlic and mushrooms and cook just for a minute. Pour the water over and close the lid. Seal by turning clockwise and choose "MANUAL" Set the cooking times to 4 minutes. Cook on HIGH pressure.

When done, do a quick pressure release. Drain the mushrooms and garlic. Transfer to a food processor. Add the lemon juice, olive oil, salt, pepper, and sesame paste. Process until smooth. Stir in the sesame seeds.

NUTRITION FACTS PER SERVING:

Calories 195, Protein 5g, Total Carbs 19g, Total Fat 8g, Saturated Fat 2g, Fiber 3g, Sodium 340mg

Lemony Cippolini Onions

PREPARATION TIME: 10 minutes **COOKING TIME:** 6 minutes **SERVES:** 6

INGREDIENTS:

1 ½ pounds Cippolini Onions, peeled
2 tbsp Lemon Juice
3 tbsp Olive Oil
½ tsp chopped Rosemary

2 Bay Leaves
1 cup Water
1 tsp Lemon Zest
Salt and Pepper, to taste

INSTRUCTIONS:

Combine the water, onions, and bay leaves in your Instant Pot. Close the lid and turn clockwise to seal. Select the "MANUAL" cooking mode. Set the cooking time to 6 minutes. Cook on HIGH pressure.

When the timer goes off, move the handle from "Sealing" to "Venting" to allow quick pressure. Drain the onions and transfer to a cutting board. Cut into quarters. Whisk together the remaining ingredients and pour over the onions.

NUTRITION FACTS PER SERVING:

Calories 130, Protein 2g, Total Carbs 19g, Total Fat 1g, Saturated Fat 0g, Fiber 3.5g, Sodium 300mg

Pico de Gallo with Carrots

PREPARATION TIME: 60 minutes **COOKING TIME:** 8 minutes **SERVES:** 6

INGREDIENTS:

1 cup chopped Onions
1 cup chopped Carrots
2 cups chopped Tomatoes
½ cup chopped Bell Peppers
2 tbsp chopped Cilantro
1 tsp minced Garlic

¼ cup Lime Juice
1 Jalapeno, deseed and minced
1 tbsp Olive Oil
½ tsp Sea Salt
¼ tsp Pepper

INSTRUCTIONS:

Turn the Instant Pot on and set it to "SAUTE". Add the olive oil and heat until sizzling. Add the onions, peppers, and carrots, and cook for 4 minutes. Add the tomatoes and cook for 3 minutes. Stir in the garlic and saute just for another minute. Transfer the mixture to a bowl and let cool for about 15 minutes.

Stir in the remaining ingredients. Cover the bowl with a plastic wrap and place it in the fridge. Let sit in the fridge for about 45 minutes before serving. Enjoy!

NUTRITION FACTS PER SERVING:

Calories 85, Protein 2g, Total Carbs 12g, Total Fat 4g, Saturated Fat 1g, Fiber 2g, Sodium 250mg

Tahini, Carrot, and Spinach "Hummus"

PREPARATION TIME: 10 minutes **COOKING TIME:** 5 minutes **SERVES:** 6

INGREDIENTS:

3 cups chopped Carrots
3 tbsp Tahini
2 cups chopped Spinach
1 Garlic Clove, crushed

2 tbsp Lemon Juice
2 tbsp Olive Oil
2 cups Water
Salt and Pepper, to taste

INSTRUCTIONS:

Combine the carrots and water in your Instant Pot. Close the lid and turn clockwise to seal. Select the "MANUAL" cooking mode. Set the cooking time to 4 minutes. Cook on HIGH pressure.

When the timer goes off, move the handle to "Venting" to release the pressure quickly. Open the lid and drain the carrots. Transfer them to a food processor. Add the remaining ingredients and process until the mixture becomes smooth.

NUTRITION FACTS PER SERVING:

Calories 170, Protein 4g, Total Carbs 17g, Total Fat 6g, Saturated Fat 2g, Fiber 3.5g, Sodium 220mg

Jalapeno and Pineapple Salsa

PREPARATION TIME: 60 minutes **COOKING TIME:** 5 minutes **SERVES:** 6

INGREDIENTS:

1 cup diced Red Onions
2 cups diced Pineapple
¼ cup chopped Cilantro
3 Jalapenos, minced

¼ tsp Garlic Powder
2 tbsp Lime Juice
¼ tsp Sea Salt
1 tbsp Coconut Oil

INSTRUCTIONS:

Turn the Instant Pot on and set it to "SAUTE". Add the coconut oil to it. When the oil becomes melted, add the onions and cook until they become softened, which should take about 3 minutes. Then, stir in the jalapenos, pineapple, and garlic powder, and cook just for 1-2 minutes. Transfer to a bowl.

In a small bowl, whisk the lime juice, pepper, and salt. Pour over the pineapples and coat to combine. Stir in cilantro. Let sit for about 15 minutes. Cover the bowl with a plastic wrap. Refrigerate for 45 minutes before serving.

NUTRITION FACTS PER SERVING:

Calories 40, Protein 0g, Total Carbs 8g, Total Fat 1g, Saturated Fat 0g, Fiber 2g, Sodium 195mg

Balsamic Carrots

INGREDIENTS:

1 pound Baby Carrots
3 tbsp Balsamic Vinegar
½ tsp Pepper
3 tbsp chopped Thyme

½ tsp Sea Salt
1 cup Olive Oil
1 tbsp Sunflower Seeds, chopped
Water, as needed

INSTRUCTIONS:

Place the carrots inside the Instant Pot. Add enough water to cover them. Close the lid and turn it clockwise to seal properly. Choose "MANUAL" after the chime. Set the cooking time to 8 minutes and cook on HIGH pressure.

When the timer goes off, press the "KEEP WARM/CANCEL" button. Turn the pressure handle from "Sealing" to "Venting" to release the pressure quickly. Open the lid gently and drain the carrots.

Place the carrots in a bowl and discard the water from the Instant Pot. Wipe the Instant Pot clean.

Set the Instant Pot to "SAUTE" and place the carrots inside. Add the rest of the ingredients and toss to coat well. Cook on "SAUTE" for about 3 minutes.

Serve and enjoy!

Nutrition facts per serving:

Calories 185, Protein 1g, Total Carbs 12g, Total Fat 15g, Saturated Fat 2g, Fiber 4g, Sodium 380mg

Turnip and Sultana Dip with Pecans

INGREDIENTS:

1 cup Water

2 pounds Turnips, peeled and chopped

½ cup Sultanas

1 tbsp Vinegar

1 tbsp Coconut Oil

¼ tsp Sea Salt

¼ tsp Pepper

INSTRUCTIONS:

Turn the Instant Pot on and press the "SAUTE" button. Add the coconut oil to it. When it becomes melted, add the parsnips. Cook them until they become softened, about 3 minutes.

Then, stir in the sultanas and water. Put the lid on and turn it clockwise to seal. Select the "MANUAL" cooking mode. Set the cooking time to 2 minutes. Cook on HIGH pressure.

Choose "KEEP WARM/CANCEL" after the beep. Move the pressure handle to "Venting" for a quick pressure release. Open the lid carefully, keeping your hands away from the steam.

Drain the parsnips and sultanas and place in a food processor. Add some of the cooking water to it, to make it creamier. Add the vinegar, salt, and pepper, and pulse until smooth. Serve topped with chopped pecans.

NUTRITION FACTS PER SERVING:

Calories 270, Protein 5g, Total Carbs 45g, Total Fat 10g, Saturated Fat 1.5g, Fiber 5g, Sodium 320mg

Pea and Avocado Dip

PREPARATION TIME: 10 minutes **COOKING TIME:** 16 minutes **SERVES:** 6

INGREDIENTS:

1 ½ cups dried Green Peas

1 tbsp Lime Juice

1 Avocado, peeled and deseeded

¼ tsp Pepper

1 Garlic Clove, peeled

2 cups Water

INSTRUCTIONS:

Combine the water and peas in the Instant Pot.

Close the lid and turn clockwise to seal.

After you hear the chime, select the "MANUAL" cooking mode.

With the "+" and "-" buttons, set the cooking time to 16 minutes.

Cook on HIGH pressure.

When the timer goes off, press the "KEEP WARM/CANCEL" button.

Release the pressure quickly by moving the handle to "Venting".

Be careful when opening the lid as the steam may burn you.

Drain the peas and transfer them to a food processor.

Add the remaining ingredients.

Pulse until smooth and creamy.

Serve and enjoy!

NUTRITION FACTS PER SERVING:

Calories 80, Protein 3g, Total Carbs 10g, Total Fat 4g, Saturated Fat 0g, Fiber 3.5g, Sodium 10mg

Turmeric Sweet Potato Sticks

PREPARATION TIME: 5 minutes **COOKING TIME:** 10 minutes **SERVES:** 1

INGREDIENTS:

1 Sweet Potato, peeled and cut into sticks

1 tbsp Coconut Oil

¼ tsp Pepper

¼ tsp Sea Salt

1 tsp Turmeric

1 ½ cups Water

INSTRUCTIONS:

Combine the water and potato stick in your Instant Pot.

Close the lid and turn it clockwise to seal.

Select "MANUAL" and set the cooking time to 5 minutes. Cook on HIGH pressure.

When the timer goes off, press the "KEEP WARM/CANCEL" button.

Move the handle to "Venting" for a quick pressure release and then open the lid carefully.

Drain the potatoes and discard the water. Wipe the Instant Pot clean.

Set the Instant Pot to "SAUTE" and add the coconut oil to it.

When melted, add the potato sticks and sprinkle with turmeric, salt, and pepper.

Saute for about 5 minutes, flipping the sticks over once.

Serve and enjoy!

NUTRITION FACTS PER SERVING:

Calories 140, Protein 1g, Total Carbs 16g, Total Fat 0g, Saturated Fat 0g, Fiber 2g, Sodium 390mg

Tropical Salsa Mash

PREPARATION TIME: 5 minutes **COOKING TIME:** 6 minutes **SERVES:** 4

INGREDIENTS:

¼ cup chopped Red Onions
1 cup chopped Mango
1 cup chopped Apples
1 cup chopped Tomatoes
1 cup diced Pineapples
2 tbsp chopped Mint
2 Jalapenos, minced

1 Garlic Clove, minced
2 tbsp chopped Cilantro
¼ cup Lime Juice
1 tbsp Olive Oil
¼ tsp Sea Salt
¼ tsp Pepper

INSTRUCTIONS:

Turn the Instant Pot on and set it to "SAUTE".

Add the olive oil to it and cook until it becomes super-hot. When sizzling, add the onions and cook for 2 minutes.

Add apples, pineapples, tomatoes, and mangos, and cook for 3 more minutes. Stir in the garlic, salt, and pepper, and cook for another minute.

Transfer the mixture to a bowl.

Stir in the remaining ingredients. Place the mixture in a food processor and pulse for just two seconds.

The mixture shouldn't be smooth, but chunky.

Serve and enjoy!

NUTRITION FACTS PER SERVING:

Calories 95, Protein 1g, Total Carbs 23g, Total Fat 0g, Saturated Fat 0g, Fiber 4g, Sodium 180mg

BREAKFAST RECIPES

Almond & Gala Apple Porridge

PREPARATION TIME: 5 minutes **COOKING TIME:** 3 minutes **SERVES:** 1

INGREDIENTS:

½ cup Almond Milk
3 tbsp ground Almonds
1 Gala Apple, grated
1 tbsp Almond Butter

2 tbsp Flaxseed
A pinch of Cinnamon
¼ tsp Vanilla Extract

INSTRUCTIONS:

Place all of the ingredients in your Instant Pot.

Give the mixture a good stir to combine the ingredients well.

Put the lid on and turn it clockwise to close it. The chiming sound should indicate proper sealing.

Hit the "MANUAL" button and set the cooking time to 5 minutes with the help of the "+" and "-" buttons. Cook on HIGH.

After the beep, press "KEEP WARM/CANCEL" to turn the Instant Pot off.

Release the pressure quickly by moving the pressure release handle from "Sealing" to "Venting".

Keep your hands away from the steam!

Stir well before serving and transfer the mixture to a serving bowl.

Enjoy!

NUTRITION FACTS PER SERVING:

Calories 445, Protein 4g, Total Carbs 40g, Total Fat 18.5g, Saturated Fat 8g, Fiber 13.2g, Sodium 34mg

Carrot & Pecan Muffins

PREPARATION TIME: 15 minutes **COOKING TIME:** 15 minutes **SERVES:** 8

INGREDIENTS:

¼ cup Coconut Oil

½ cup Almond Milk

½ cup chopped Pecans

1 tsp Apple Pie Spice

1 cup shredded Carrots

3 Eggs

⅓ cup Pure & Organic Applesauce

1 cup ground Almonds

1 ½ cups Water

INSTRUCTIONS:

Pour the water into the IP and lower the trivet.

Place the coconut oil, almond milk, eggs, applesauce, almonds and apple pie spice, in a large mixing bowl.

Beat the mixture well with an electric mixer, until it becomes fluffy. Fold in the carrots and pecans.

Pour the batter into 8 silicone muffin cups and arrange them on top of the trivet.

Put the lid on and turn it clockwise to close it.

After you hear the chime, press "MANUAL" button and set the cooking time to 15 minutes.

When the timer goes off, hit "KEEP WARM/CANCEL" to turn the Instant Pot off. Move the pressure release handle from "Sealing" to "Venting" to do a quick pressure release.

Carefully open the lid. Remove the muffins.

NUTRITION FACTS PER SERVING:

Calories 265, Protein 6g, Total Carbs 6g, Total Fat 25g, Saturated Fat 13g, Fiber 3g, Sodium 250mg

Kale, Tomato & Carrot Quiche

PREPARATION TIME: 10 minutes **COOKING TIME:** 20 minutes **SERVES:** 4

INGREDIENTS:

1 Large Carrot, shredded
1 Large Tomato, chopped
½ cup chopped Kale
¼ cup Almond Milk
¼ Onion, diced
½ Bell Pepper, diced

1 tsp Basil
Pinch of Pepper
¼ tsp Paprika
8 Eggs
1 ½ cups Water

INSTRUCTIONS:

Pour the water into your Instant Pot and lower the trivet.

Place the eggs, almond milk, pepper, basil, and paprika, in a large bowl.

Whisk until well combined and smooth.

Add the veggies to the mixture and stir well to combine.

Grease a baking dish with some cooking spray and pour the egg and veggie mixture into it.

Place the baking dish on top of the trivet and put the lid of the IP on. Press "MANUAL" and then set the cooking time to 20 minutes with the help of the "+" and "-" buttons. Cook on HIGH pressure.

After the beep, press "KEEP WARM/CANCEL" and let the pressure come down on its own. Open carefully the lid once the pressure valve has dropped down.

Remove the quiche from the Instant Pot.

Serve and enjoy!

NUTRITION FACTS PER SERVING:

Calories 170, Protein 13.5g, Total Carbs 6.5g, Total Fat 10g, Saturated Fat 5g, Fiber 1.4g, Sodium 220mg

Sweet Potato & Carrot Egg Casserole

PREPARATION TIME: 5 minutes **COOKING TIME:** 10 minutes **SERVES:** 4

INGREDIENTS:

8 Eggs
½ cup Almond Milk
2 cups shredded Sweet Potatoes
1 cup shredded Carrots
½ tbsp Olive Oil

½ tsp dried Parsley
¼ tsp Pepper
¼ tsp Paprika
¼ tsp Garlic Powder

INSTRUCTIONS:

Add the olive oil to the Instant Pot and set it to "SAUTE".

When the oil becomes hot and sizzling, add the carrots and sweet potatoes.

Add the herbs and spices, stir well to combine, and cook the veggies for about 2-3 minutes.

Meanwhile, beat together the eggs and almond milk in a bowl.

Pour the mixture over the carrots and stir to incorporate well.

Put the lid on and turn it clockwise to seal.

After the chime, hit "MANUAL". Set the cooking time to 7 minutes and cook on HIGH.

Press "KEEP WARM/CANCEL" after you hear the beep to turn the Instant Pot off.

Move the pressure release handle from "Sealing" to "Venting" to do a quick pressure release and open the lid carefully.

Serve and enjoy!

NUTRITION FACTS PER SERVING:

Calories 220, Protein 6g, Total Carbs 17.2g, Total Fat 7g, Saturated Fat 4g, Fiber 2g, Sodium 340mg

Onion and Tomato Eggs

PREPARATION TIME: 10 minutes **COOKING TIME:** 8 minutes **SERVES:** 2

INGREDIENTS:

4 Eggs
1 Tomato, chopped
1 Red Onion, diced
¼ tsp Garlic Powder

Pinch of Cayenne Pepper
Pinch of Black Pepper
1 ½ cups Water

INSTRUCTIONS:

Pour the water into the Instant Pot and lower the trivet.

Grease a baking dish with some cooking spray.

Beat the eggs along with the garlic powder, cayenne, and black pepper.

Add tomatoes and onions and stir to combine well.

Pour the mixture into the greased baking dish.

Place the baking dish on top of the trivet and close the lid.

Turn clockwise to seal and press "MANUAL". Cook on HIGH for 8 minutes.

After the beep, press "KEEP WARM/CANCEL".

When the Instant Pot is off, move the pressure release handle from "Sealing" to "Venting" to do a quick pressure release.

Open the lid carefully and remove the baking dish from the pot.

Serve and enjoy!

NUTRITION FACTS PER SERVING:

Calories 380, Protein 15g, Total Carbs 13g, Total Fat 16g, Saturated Fat 9.2g, Fiber 3g, Sodium 410mg

Bell Pepper & Onion Frittata

PREPARATION TIME: 7 minutes **COOKING TIME:** 8 minutes **SERVES:** 2

INGREDIENTS:

3 Eggs
¼ cup diced Bell Pepper
¼ cup diced Onion
2 tbsp Almond Milk

¼ tsp Garlic Powder
Pinch of Turmeric Powder
1 ½ cups Water

INSTRUCTIONS:

Pour the water into the Instant Pot and lower the trivet. Grease a small baking dish with some cooking spray.

In a bowl, beat the eggs along with the almond milk, turmeric, and garlic powder.

Add onions and bell peppers and stir well to combine.

Pour the mixture into the greased baking dish and place it on top of the trivet.

Close the lid of the Instant Pot and turn it clockwise. The chiming sound means it is sealed properly.

Select "MANUAL" and set the cooking time to 8 minutes. Cook on HIGH.

After the timer goes off, press "KEEP WARM/CANCEL" to turn the Instant Pot off.

Release the pressure quickly by moving the pressure release handle from "Sealing" to "Venting".

Keep your hands away from the steam to avoid burning yourself.

Carefully open the lid and remove the dish from the pot.

Serve and enjoy!

NUTRITION FACTS PER SERVING:

Calories 240, Protein 15g, Total Carbs 6g, Total Fat 16g, Saturated Fat 8g, Fiber 2g, Sodium 350mg

Egg and Beef Casserole with Kale and Leek

PREPARATION TIME: 10 minutes **COOKING TIME:** 30 minutes **SERVES:** 4

INGREDIENTS:

8 ounces ground Beef

6 eggs, beaten

¾ cup Sliced Leeks

¾ cup chopped Kale

1 Sweet Potato, peeled and shredded

1 Garlic Clove, minced

1 tbsp Coconut Oil

Pinch of Pepper

1 ½ cups Water

INSTRUCTIONS:

Grease a baking dish with some cooking spray and set aside.

Add the coconut oil to the Instant Pot and set it to "SAUTE". When melted, add the leeks and cook for about 2 minutes.

Add the garlic and cook for 30 seconds or so. Add the beef and cook for a few more minutes, until browned.

Transfer to a bowl. Add the remaining ingredients and stir well to combine.

Pour the water into the Instant Pot and lower the trivet. Pour the egg and beef mixture into the greased baking dish and place on top of the trivet.

Close the lid and turn clockwise to seal. Select "MANUAL" and set the cooking time to 25 minutes. Cook on HIGH.

After the beep, press "KEEP WARM/CANCEL" to turn the Instant Pot off.

Release the pressure quickly by moving the handle to "Venting". Be careful not to burn yourself and open the lid.

Remove the baking dish from the pot carefully.

Serve and enjoy!

NUTRITION FACTS PER SERVING:

Calories 420, Protein 24g, Total Carbs 13g, Total Fat 30g, Saturated Fat 15g, Fiber 1.6g, Sodium 420mg

Easy Soft-Boiled Eggs

PREPARATION TIME: 3 minutes **COOKING TIME:** 7 minutes **SERVES:** 4

INGREDIENTS:

8 Eggs   1 cup of Water

INSTRUCTIONS:

Pour the water into the Instant Pot and place the eggs inside. Put the lid on and turn it clockwise to seal. After you hear the chime, press the "MANUAL" button. Cook on HIGH pressure for 3 minutes.

After you hear the beeping sound, press "KEEP WARM/CANCEL" and turn the Instant Pot off. Do a quick pressure release by moving the handle from "Sealing" to "Venting". Open the lid and be careful not to put your hands near the steam.

Prepare an ice bath and drop the hardboiled eggs into it to speed up the process of cooling. Serve and enjoy!

NUTRITION FACTS PER SERVING:

Calories 140, Protein 12g, Total Carbs 2g, Total Fat 9g, Saturated Fat 3g, Fiber 0g, Sodium 130mg

Pear, Coconut & Walnut Porridge

PREPARATION TIME: 3 minutes **COOKING TIME:** 3 minutes **SERVES:** 1

INGREDIENTS:

½ cup ground Walnuts   1 Pear, diced
1 ounces Coconut Flakes   ½ cup Coconut Milk

INSTRUCTIONS:

Place all of the ingredients in your Instant Pot and stir well to combine. Put the lid on. Turn clockwise to seal, and after you hear the chime hit "MANUAL". Use the "+" and "-" buttons and set the cooking time to 3 minutes. Make sure to cook on HIGH pressure.

When the timer goes off, press "KEEP WARM/CANCEL" and move the handle to "Venting" for a quick pressure release. Open the lid but keep your hands away from the steam to avoid burning. Transfer the mixture to a serving bowl and stir once again to combine. Enjoy!

NUTRITION FACTS PER SERVING:

Calories 568, Protein 9g, Total Carbs 37.6g, Total Fat 48g, Saturated Fat 21.7g, Fiber 11g, Sodium 25mg

Eggs & Smoked Salmon

PREPARATION TIME: 5 minutes **COOKING TIME:** 3 minutes **SERVES:** 1

INGREDIENTS:

4 slices of Smoked Salmon
4 Eggs
1 tsp chopped Cilantro

Pinch of Paprika
Pinch of Pepper
1 cup of Water

INSTRUCTIONS:

Pour the water into the Instant Pot and lower the trivet. Grease 4 ramekins with some cooking spray or olive oil. If using silicone ramekins, skip this step.

Place a slice of smoked salmon at the bottom of each ramekin. Crack an egg on top of the salmon. Season with pepper and paprika and sprinkle with the cilantro. Arrange the ramekins on top of the trivet and close the lid. Turn it clockwise to seal it and then press "MANUAL" after you hear the chime. Set the cooking time to 5 minutes and cook on HIGH.

After the timer goes off, press "KEEP WARM/CANCEL" to turn the Instant Pot off. Release the pressure quickly by moving the pressure release handle from "Sealing" to "Venting". Keep your hands away from the steam to avoid burning yourself.

NUTRITION FACTS PER SERVING:

Calories 240, Protein 19g, Total Carbs 2g, Total Fat 17g, Saturated Fat 12g, Fiber 0g, Sodium 280mg

DESSERT RECIPES

Cinnamon and Lemon Apples

PREPARATION TIME: 10 minutes **COOKING TIME:** 3 minutes **SERVES:** 2

INGREDIENTS:

2 Apples, peeled and cut into wedges   1 tbsp Almond Butter
½ cup Lemon Juice   1 cup Water
½ tsp Cinnamon

INSTRUCTIONS:

Combine the lemon juice and water in the Instant Pot.

Place the apple wedges inside the steaming basket and lower the basket into the Instant Pot.

Close the lid and turn clockwise to seal. Select the "MANUAL" cooking mode.

Set the cooking time to 3 minutes. Cook on HIGH pressure.

When the timer goes off, press the "KEEP WARM/CANCEL" button.

Turn the pressure handle from "Sealing" to "Venting" to release the pressure quickly.

Open the lid and remove the steaming basket.

Transfer the apple wedges to a bowl.

Drizzle with almond butter and sprinkle with cinnamon.

Serve and enjoy!

NUTRITION FACTS PER SERVING:

Calories 144, Protein 2g, Total Carbs 25g, Total Fat 5.5g, Saturated Fat 1g, Fiber 5g, Sodium 85mg

Chocolate and Almond Banana Squares

PREPARATION TIME: 10 minutes **COOKING TIME:** 15 minutes **SERVES:** 6

INGREDIENTS:

½ cup Almond Butter
3 Bananas
2 tbsp Cocoa Powder
1 ½ cups Water

INSTRUCTIONS:

Place the bananas and almond butter in a bowl and mash them finely with a fork. Add the cocoa powder and stir until well combined.

Grab a baking dish that can fit into the Instant Pot and grease it with some cooking spray. Pour the banana and almond batter into the dish.

Pour the water into the Instant Pot and lower the trivet. Place the baking dish on top of the trivet and put the lid of the Instant Pot on.

Turn it clockwise to seal and then select the "MANUAL" cooking mode. Set the cooking time to 15 minutes. Cook on HIGH pressure.

When the timer goes off, press the "KEEP WARM/CANCEL" button. Turn the handle to "Venting" and release the pressure quickly.

Open the lid and take out the baking dish. Let cool for a few minutes before cutting into squares. Serve and enjoy!

NUTRITION FACTS PER SERVING:

Calories 140, Protein 3g, Total Carbs 14g, Total Fat 10g, Saturated Fat 2g, Fiber 2g, Sodium 70mg

Very Berry Cream

PREPARATION TIME: 4 hours 10 minutes **COOKING TIME:** 2 minutes
SERVES: 2

INGREDIENTS:

⅓ cup Blueberries
⅓ cup chopped Strawberries
⅓ cup Raspberries

1 cup Coconut Milk
¼ tsp Vanilla Extract

INSTRUCTIONS:

Place all of the ingredients, except the vanilla extract, inside your Instant Pot. Close the lid and turn it clockwise to seal. Select the "MANUAL" cooking mode and set the cooking time to 2 minutes. Make sure to cook on HIGH pressure.

When the timer goes off, press "KEEP WARM/CANCEL". Turn the pressure handle to "Venting" for a quick pressure release and open the lid carefully. Transfer the mixture to a blender.

Add the vanilla extract and pulse until smooth. Divide between two serving glasses and place in the fridge. Refrigerate for 4 hours before serving. Enjoy!

NUTRITION FACTS PER SERVING:

Calories 90, Protein 1g, Total Carbs 10.5g, Total Fat 3.5g, Saturated Fat 0g, Fiber 2g, Sodium 50mg

Coconut Pear Delight

PREPARATION TIME: 10 minutes **COOKING TIME:** 5 minutes **SERVES:** 2

INGREDIENTS:

¼ cup Almond Flour
1 cup Coconut Milk
2 Large Pears, peeled and diced
¼ cup Shredded Coconut,

unsweetened

INSTRUCTIONS:

Combine all of the ingredients in your Instant Pot. Close the lid and turn clockwise to seal. Select "MANUAL" and set the cooking time to 5 minutes. Cook on HIGH pressure.

After the beep, press the "KEEP WARM/CANCEL" button. Turn the pressure handle to "Venting" so you can allow a quick pressure release.

Open the lid very carefully, keeping your hands away from the steam. Divide the mixture between two bowls. Sprinkle with some cinnamon, if desired. Enjoy!

NUTRITION FACTS PER SERVING:

Calories 140, Protein 2g, Total Carbs 18g, Total Fat 8g, Saturated Fat 2g, Fiber 3g, Sodium 80mg

Creamy Almond and Coconut Apple Dessert

PREPARATION TIME: 10 minutes **COOKING TIME:** 4 minutes **SERVES:** 4

INGREDIENTS:

3 Apples, peeled and diced   ½ cup Coconut Milk
½ cup chopped or slivered Almonds   ¼ tsp Cinnamon

INSTRUCTIONS:

Place all of the ingredients inside your Instant Pot. Stir well to combine and put the lid on. Turn the lid clockwise to seal and press the "MANUAL" button. Set the cooking time to 4 minutes. Cook on HIGH pressure.

When the timer goes off, press the "KEEP WARM/CANCEL" button. Moe the handle from "Sealing" to "Venting" to release the pressure quickly. Open the lid gently and divide the mixture between 4 serving bowls. Enjoy!

NUTRITION FACTS PER SERVING:

Calories 60, Protein 0g, Total Carbs 10g, Total Fat 1g, Saturated Fat 0g, Fiber 2g, Sodium 10mg

Almond Pear Wedges

PREPARATION TIME: 8 minutes **COOKING TIME:** 7 minutes **SERVES:** 3

INGREDIENTS:

2 Large Pears, peeled and cut into wedges

3 tbsp Almond Butter

2 tbsp Coconut Oil

INSTRUCTIONS:

Pour 1 cup of water into the Instant Pot. Place the pear wedges in a steamer basket and then lower the basket into the pot. Close the lid and turn clockwise to seal. Press "MANUAL" and set the cooking time to 2 minutes. Cook on HIGH.

When the timer goes off, move the pressure handle to "Venting" for a quick pressure release. Open the lid carefully and take out the basket. Discard the water and wipe the Instant Pot clean. Press "SAUTE" and add in the coconut oil. When melted, add the pears and cook until browned. Top with butter and serve.

NUTRITION FACTS PER SERVING:

Calories 240, Protein 1g, Total Carbs 22g, Total Fat 17g, Saturated Fat 4g, Fiber 6g, Sodium 80mg

Black Currant Poached Peaches

PREPARATION TIME: 10 minutes **COOKING TIME:** 5 minutes **SERVES:** 4

INGREDIENTS:

½ cup Black Currants

4 Peaches, peeled, pits removed

1 cup Freshly Squeezed Orange Juice

1 Cinnamon Stick

INSTRUCTIONS:

Place the black currants and the orange juice in a blender. Blend until the mixture becomes smooth. Pour the orange/currant mixture into your Instant Pot. Add the cinnamon stick inside. Place the peaches inside the steamer basket.

Lower the basket into the pot. Close the lid and turn clockwise to seal. Select the "MANUAL" mode. Set the cooking time to 5 minutes. Cook on HIGH pressure.

Press the "KEEP WARM/CANCEL" button after you hear the beep. Turn the pressure handle to "Venting" for a quick pressure release and open the lid carefully. Serve the peaches drizzled with the sauce. Enjoy!

NUTRITION FACTS PER SERVING:

Calories 140, Protein 1g, Total Carbs 15g, Total Fat 1g, Saturated Fat 0g, Fiber 3g, Sodium 25mg

Apple and Peach Compote

PREPARATION TIME: 2 hours and 10 minutes **COOKING TIME:** 8 minutes
SERVES: 4

INGREDIENTS:

2 ½ cups Peach pieces
2 cups diced Apples
Juice of 1 Orange

2 tbsp Arrowroot
½ cup Water
¼ tsp Cinnamon

INSTRUCTIONS:

Place the peaches, apples, water, and orange juice, inside the Instant Pot. Stir to combine and close the lid. Turn the lid clockwise to seal properly. Select the "MANUAL" cooking mode and set the cooking time to 3 minutes. Cook on HIGH pressure.

Select "KEEP WARM/CANCEL" after the beep. Turn the pressure handle to "Venting" for a quick pressure release and open the lid carefully.

Press the "SAUTE" button and whisk in the arrowroot. Cook until the compote is thickened, about 5 minutes or so. Transfer the compote to an airtight container. Refrigerate for about 2 hours. Serve and enjoy!

NUTRITION FACTS PER SERVING:

Calories 120, Protein 1g, Total Carbs 23g, Total Fat 1g, Saturated Fat 0g, Fiber 6.5g, Sodium 50mg

Tutty Fruity Sauce

PREPARATION TIME: 10 minutes **COOKING TIME:** 5 minutes **SERVES:** 2

INGREDIENTS:

1 cup Pineapple Chunks
1 cup Berry Mix
2 Apples, peeled and diced

¼ cup chopped Almonds
¼ cup Fresh Orange Juice
1 tbsp Coconut Oil

INSTRUCTIONS:

Place ⅔ cup of water, the orange juice, and fruits, inside the Instant Pot. Give the mixture a good stir and put the lid on.

Turn clockwise to seal. Press "MANUAL" and set the cooking time to 5 minutes. Cook on HIGH pressure.

When the timer goes off, press the "KEEP WARM/CANCEL" button. Turn the pressure handle to "Venting" and release the pressure quickly.

Blend the mixture with a hand blender and immediately stir in the coconut oil. Serve sprinkled with chopped almonds. Enjoy!

NUTRITION FACTS PER SERVING:

Calories 125, Protein 1g, Total Carbs 16g, Total Fat 4g, Saturated Fat 1g, Fiber 4g, Sodium 25mg

Almond Butter Bananas

INGREDIENTS:

1 Banana, sliced

1 tbsp Almond Butter

2 tbsp Coconut Butter

½ tsp Cinnamon

INSTRUCTIONS:

Turn the Instant Pot on and set it to "SAUTE". Add the coconut oil to it and cook until it becomes melted.

Add the banana slices and "fry" them for a couple of minutes, or until they become golden on both sides.

Top the fried bananas with almond butter and sprinkle with some cinnamon over. Serve and enjoy!

NUTRITION FACTS PER SERVING:

Calories 310, Protein 2g, Total Carbs 28g, Total Fat 23g, Saturated Fat 5g, Fiber 3g, Sodium 70mg

CONCLUSION

I hope that this book was able to realize that eating healthy and cleansing foods that can help you lose weight can actually be fun and yummy. Having these 100 delightful meals in your recipe folder, you are more than equipped to start your 30 Days Whole Foods journey without worrying that you will be tempted to sneak some junk foods into your diet.

Sounds too good to be true? Try these recipes now and see what I am talking about. Your dreamy figure will thank you later. And so will your taste buds!

Made in the USA
Coppell, TX
13 December 2020